THE COMING
MIDEAST WAR
AND PEACE TREATY

THE COMING
MIDEAST WAR
AND PEACE TREATY

DAVID BRENNAN

**The Coming Mideast War
and Peace Treaty**

The Unfolding Prophetic Puzzle

Published by Teknon Publishing, Metairie, Louisiana.

ISBN Number: 978-0-9887614-1-4

*Acknowledgment: It is a pleasure to acknowledge the pro-
fessional copy-editing done by Sue Hatfield-Green.*

Table of Contents

CHAPTER ONE

When They Say "Peace" in the Mideast

Across the entire globe it is in the tiny region called Palestine where the three major religions of the world experienced their beginning: Judaism, Christianity and Islam. Early within the Holy Bible we are told that a great split occurred which eventually resulted in this division of faith. It all began with the "friend" of God, Abraham, whose lineage would form the basis of all three religions. God assured Abraham that one son, Ishmael, will become a great people. But as for the other son, "my covenant I shall establish with Isaac."[1] He would make it clear that only Isaac, fathered by Abraham, and mothered by his wife, Sarah, could become the true heir. And from Isaac the Lord would enter into a covenant, producing a "kingdom of priests and holy nation."[2,3] That nation would be Israel.

Whereas Ishmael entered the world by natural means, procreated by Abraham through his maid servant, the basis of his birth would rest on a lack of faith in a previous promise from God that he would finally have a son. Since his wife was so old, he decided that a natural means was necessary to accomplish God's promise. As a result, the household maid was chosen the produce him a child, which resulted in Ishmael. However, Sarah, although very old, amazingly, would become pregnant with Isaac, his birth coming from the supernatural. So it was a result of that supernatural beginning that the nation of Israel would eventually come into being. Thereafter, Israel would experience an array of supernatural events, signs, and warnings as a matter of the norm. On the other hand, the descendents of Ishmael would form the Arab peoples of the Middle East whom would, eventually, embrace Islam and make themselves the implacable enemies of the descendents of Isaac—-the Jews found in Israel today. That ancient split is centered on Palestine, and is the focal point of modern religious conflict, pitting the Christians and Jews against the Muslims. And in spite of all political protestations to the contrary, it is truly a great religious conflict playing out.

Since the birth of Israel in 1948, and the attendant conflict with the ancestors of Ishmael that started up again in that year, it has been the dream of American presidents to bring about a true and lasting peace to the troubled region. And in spite of the tremendous power and prestige of that office, such an accomplishment has been the impossible Gordian knot to untie. President Jimmy Carter would loosen part of it, amazingly, with a peace treaty between Israel and Egypt, convincing the Jews it was in their best interest to return the giant Sinai desert to their foe, in return for diplomatic relations and a demilitarization of the region.[3] And until the Muslim Brotherhood replaced the friendly regime of Egyptian President Hosni Mubarak in 2010, it appeared to work. But that now appears to be unraveling.

With the elevation of Barack Obama to the United States presidency, and his unique background, this book will present the case that a confluence of Scripture and events have come together which are indicating that the much-coveted peace agreement is approaching. Having received the Nobel Peace Prize early in his first term for peace accomplishments not yet accomplished, the Nobel committee's actions were, perhaps, prophetic. This book will look at how supernatural times appear to once again have arrived on Earth, and how Israel, naturally, is the focal point of it all. It will also look at how the rise of President Obama was, if it was anything, highly unusual, leading to the most sensible question begging to be asked: If so, then why at this moment in time? But there is much more.

There has evolved a constellation of events surrounding Israel which has caused it to be placed in the most vulnerable position since its war for independence. Now in an Obama second term that many feared would unleash an unrestrained withdrawal of support from Israel, the surprising opposite has initially occurred. But instead of representing a welcomed change of heart toward the tiny nation, it has the ominous undercurrent of something carefully choreographed beyond the means of the natural. As this sequence of geopolitical events is lining up in a way that indicates incredible intellect at work, it is accompanied by other supernatural signs unfolding in the heavens above, alerting those who understand the ancient warnings of an approaching great event relative to Israel.

There are signs in the heavens that have begun unfolding in 2013, and destined to reach their crescendo in 2014 and 2015, which appear to be a precise fulfillment of certain signs which passages in the Bible indicate would eventually unfold. Those warnings, however, appear to fit perfectly with other warnings since 1991 that have been playing like a broken record, indicating that their culmination is near. And these multiple warnings coming from different directions appear to be coming together at the same time, with all pointing toward the same event: a peace treaty that should bring a fulfillment of it all.

It also appears that the entire concept of "wars and rumors of wars" is now fulfilled perfectly, but in a way that was not previously understood. It is also clear that the verses referring to such "rumors of wars" mark a certain prophetic time frame in the scheme of it all, a clear demarcation that is soon to be followed by the beginning of the next phase of the "times." And the end of the "rumors of wars" can only come about by actual war.

This book will seek to lay out a series of events, some of which initially appear unconnected, and bring them together to support the notion that not only is a Middle East war between Israel and Iran near, but that a major Middle East peace agreement between Israel and the Palestinians is as well. And that such an agreement will come about from an unlikely series of events, with the appearance of having been intelligently choreographed. Additionally, with the evidence, both Scriptural and geopolitical presented here relating to Matthew 24:6-8, an array of additional prophetic Scriptures begin fitting together in what appears to be real harmony. And this understanding would be difficult to grasp until recent years. As those ancient writings come together, they appear to pinpoint exactly where the world currently is in prophecy, allowing the reader to understand the sequence of prophetic events that should unfold if the thesis here is correct. That bold statement will be supported in the chapters titled, "Wars and Rumors of Wars," and "The Sequence of Prophetic Events." But before that, it is necessary to set the stage by providing an assortment of information. If that information might appear unconnected at first, by the end of the book it should fit together nicely.

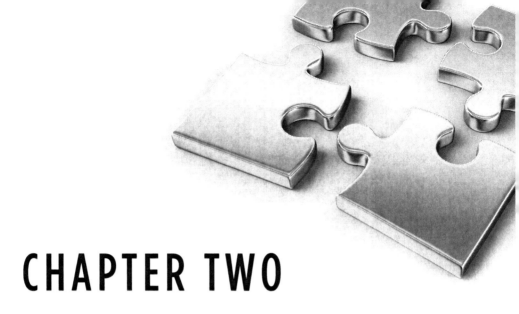

CHAPTER TWO

Supernatural Times

As the crowd of mourners stared at the large stone carefully placed to cover the opening to the cave, their collective emotion of grief now began to mix with confusion. Soon that state of mind would morph into one of stunned amazement. They remembered their friend Lazarus' sudden illness and the speed with which he had passed away. However, today the man called Jesus had arrived at the home of the grieving family. With sadness marking his face, it was clear to all the emotion he felt toward the dearly departed. And no doubt many had already heard about this Jesus. Indeed, it was almost impossible not to have heard about him.

He had been walking the countryside for a length of time accompanied by His followers, preaching a noble unction to the multitudes that was gaining increasing attention. Reports of miracles taking place at almost all of his gatherings were now so prevalent as to be common knowledge in the region. But on this day, His journey took Him to the home of Mary and Martha, the surviving sisters of Lazarus. And at Jesus' request the party of grievers found themselves back again at the tomb where Lazarus' body had been placed, with a large stone sealing the entrance. However, this man of miracles now made another request, and it was one that stirred confusion in all present. He asked that the large stone be moved aside from the tomb, exposing the rotting corpse within.[1]

Most likely, two thoughts coursed through the minds of those present on that day long ago. The first was voiced by one of Lazarus' sisters who pointed out that the body "has been there four days."[2] And there is little doubt that with that knowledge came the attendant understanding of what their collective sense of smell was about to experience. And this, certainly, had to cause many to question the strange request. But others present must have experienced a sense that disrespect was being shown to their departed friend. It was, after all, a brutal request.

However, it is apparent that Jesus' powerful reputation won the day, and with it the incredibly strange request to disturb the peace of the dead was granted. And then in a moment that had to make some cringe, to the one within the cave who could no longer hear, Jesus spoke, "Lazarus, come out."[3]

And he did.

Any present who had questioned the reports of miracles concerning this Jesus, which had been coming in from the countryside, no longer had such doubts to deal with. Instead, now they had to face the challenge of twisting their minds around what they had just seen. And it probably wasn't easy. But for whatever reason, it was given to those present to live within a time marked by grand miracles. That period of time also happened to mark the most profound of biblical times—-the much-awaited coming of the messiah. The litany of miracles included not only the dead coming back to life, but the blind seeing, the lame being healed, and such an array of other events as to cause the mind to go on tilt.[4] In that day, those who studied the ancient writings for a similar time would find it necessary to reach deep into the past to find one that even remotely compared.

Such a time would be recorded in the old texts of the Jewish Torah and focus on the strange and unusual events that surfaced in Egypt many years earlier. It was the time that the Jews were held captive there, soon to journey to the Promised Land. Such strange occurrences included the sky darkening and the river turning to blood, among other things.[5] Not only would those strange events be biblically recorded, but events eerily similar would be discovered on an ancient Egyptian papyrus found in 1822 near the pyramids of Saqqara. It is referred to as the Papyrus Ipuwer and is catalogued as "Leiden 344" at the Museum of Antiquities in the Netherlands.[6] This old scroll recorded strange and catastrophic events, from the Egyptian perspective, that coincide with those recorded in the Book of Exodus. They would include the river turning to blood, "The River is blood," and the sky darkening, "The land is without light," along with a multitude of other recordings of events coinciding to the plagues described in the Book of Exodus.[7]

So it was that after the time of Jesus and this Lazarus had passed, so too did the time of grand miracles, with the world returning to "normal" again. And with the passing of many centuries so too would pass, for many people, the belief that such things had ever really happened. However, one thing seems certain. In the days when Jesus walked the Earth, those miracles that accompanied Him were a kind of supernatural billboard erected by the Divine to advertise that the Messiah had finally arrived.

And so there the subject of strange events rested for about 2,000 years, relegated to biblical times past. But there is an observation that needs to be made about such strange times. With much banter all about that some grand biblical event in this day is on the verge of unfolding, surely for it all to be true, should there not be strange events before its arrival as in olden days? Certainly, if a biblical event of great magnitude is on the horizon, then the pattern of supernatural and astronomical events should happen again. Like the time when Lazarus greatly benefited from the human voice of Jesus, the beginning of the "times" warned of in the Bible should be marked by great and strange events.

Our Times

The prophecies indicating the nation of Israel would be re-created again in the land of their ancestors were thought by many to be allegorical or symbolic and not a literal prophecy to be looked for by the followers of Jesus. In line with that reasoning, many made elaborate attempts to explain it into something that was more reasonable and acceptable. After all, it had been about 2,000 years since Israel had existed as a nation, making the likelihood of it being reconstituted remote. The chance of such a dispersed people coming back together to form themselves into a country again was considered, by many, as too far-fetched to be a literal prophecy. Then in the year 1948, after almost two millennia of being scattered, it happened, and in the most unlikely way.

It is one thing for a people to begin a process of knitting themselves together again over the course of years, collectively and methodically gathering the means to accomplish the great task of forming a new nation. But it is another thing when about half of them had just been killed by a madman, and only a few years earlier.

With the reconstituted state of Israel back after a 2,000-year hiatus, along with it arrived the possibility that supernatural "times" could possibly be at hand once again. In fact, the reappearance of Israel was so incredible as to be supernatural. And since that much-prophesized event unfolded, other old prophecy appears to be as well. With the Jews retaking Jerusalem in 1967, that city has become the growing "cup of trembling"[8] it was destined to become for the entire world, as prophesized in the ancient Scriptures. It is, indeed, the focal point of world conflict, with the Palestinians declaring it their eternal capital, and Israel doing the same. As the Palestinian effort toward nationhood in the land biblically promised to the Jews progresses, it comes at a time when other uncanny events are unfolding.

Just as the prophecies of the coming Messiah proceeded the time that Jesus walked the Earth, the unfolding of an ancient biblical warning appears to be happening in this day. From an obscure Scripture in the Book of Isaiah, chapter 9, verses 8-12, there appears to have unfolded the most unlikely biblical warning to America. Since the sudden events of September 11, 2001, this Scripture has come to life. In his book *The Harbinger*, Jonathan Cahn explores the eerie litany of biblical warnings that have sprung forth from that horrific September day. The Scripture provides the reader with a litany of detailed warnings given to Israel many years ago, at a point in time in which the Jews had moved far away from God. The warning came in the form of an incursion against their nation by an enemy. It wasn't a full-scale invasion, just a destructive localized event. But its success was meant to shock them back to their God. However, they missed the Divine warning and continued on their previous ungodly course. Then, since they did not turn back to God, something vastly worse happened.[9] But this time the warning is not directed toward modern Israel, but to the only other nation dedicated to God at its founding: America.

In the case of the Isaiah 9 warnings, fulfilled in detail on September 11, 2001, and its aftermath, there is an eeriness associated with it that grows as it unfolds. There are nine "harbingers" within it to be exact. These "harbingers" were represented by the combining of unlikely events, such as specific words spoken by political leaders, a specific type of tree being cast down in the attack and replaced by another specific type of tree, and so forth.[10] It is an array of occurrences, which their unfolding in the correct sequence is virtually impossible to happen, save for Divine intervention. And all nine happened in the required order, and took place on the ground where America was dedicated to God by the Founding Fathers. As such, it appears that America was taken back to its ground of dedication to receive the warning. Unless all of it was nothing more than a massive conspiracy of coincidences, it constitutes a strange event in our time. To put it in simple terms, the fulfillment of this warning is so unlikely that its occurring appears to be a supernatural warning to America that she has moved too far from God.

"Peace" Treaty Efforts

Something else strange has been happening which began in the year 1991. In what appears to be another warning to America and, in this case, also to the world, a long series of "coincidences" appears to have unfolded relating to the rebirth of Israel. It too has arrived by calamity in the form of historical disasters coinciding to diplomatic efforts to remove this restored Promised Land from the Jews. Since the land was prophesized to be restored to the reconstituted nation of Israel, diplomatic efforts to remove it are effectively an effort to reverse that biblical promise, even though such efforts are being done in the name of "peace." Yet, as unlikely as it is, since 1991 thirteen historically significant disasters, covered within *The Israel Omen* and *The Israel Omen II,* coincided with those efforts to remove the land, with most occurring on the exact day that the effort took place.[11] (All are covered in Appendix A) So unlikely is such a series of "coincidences" to occur, that it places the skeptic in a position of having to choose between one of two choices to explain them. One option is to claim they are, again, nothing more than a massive conspiracy of coincidences. But as their litany grows, that option becomes increasingly difficult to sustain. The other is to recognize that something strange is occurring that qualifies as supernatural and carries with it another warning from the Divine. But there is something else strange that appears to have begun unfolding.

For those of you who have read *The Israel Omen*, what is found within the final chapter, titled "The Next Catastrophe" is a brazen attempt at forecasting a future catastrophe based on some future political action. There is a "matrix" designed to accomplish the task. This "matrix," referred to as the Political-Catastrophe-Matrix, looks at the ten events covered within that book and extracts what appear to be three distinct political triggers associated within them. Then, on that basis it goes on to speculate as to what kind of actions on the part of the Obama Administration (which at that time had just taken office) should coincide with a historically significant disaster. This, at the top of page 171 ...

> The first effort [of the Obama Administration] should break new ground, probably marked by some grand gathering of the Quartet. Another "Matrix" action could be a major shift in U.S. policy against Israel ...[12]

It is one thing to study past historical disasters for political "triggers" common to calamity. But it is another thing for future events to confirm those triggers. And, in fact, both observations on page 171 were fulfilled with eerie success.

In the quote, the reader was led to look for the Obama Administration to break new ground against the Promised Land. Essentially, it looked for an action that had never before been accomplished, and on April 20, 2010, that is exactly what happened. After months of pressuring Israel to suspend construction in East Jerusalem as a precondition for negotiations to begin, the Jewish State ceded to those demands, effectively reducing their control in the Holy City for the first time since 1967. However, on that same day, something else of note took place: British Petroleum's "Deep Water Horizon" rig exploded in the Gulf of Mexico.[13]

This coincidence fulfilled the first trigger.

The second political action indicated on page 171 led the reader to look for a major shift in U.S. policy against Israel. Indeed, on May 19,

2011, the president accommodated the "Matrix" with just that. So oner-
ous against Israel was his new policy that a group of his strongest supporters immediately came out against it, including Senate Majority leader
Harry Reed. But the most significant opposition came from Mr. Obama's
Middle East point man, George Mitchell, in the form of his resignation.
However, coinciding with that drastic policy change began what weather
experts say was the worst tornado rampage in world history, fulfilling the
other trigger indicated to look for.[14] In addition to these strange coincidences, something else appears to be unfolding directly from the pages of
the Bible.

In the Book of Zechariah, near the end of the first chapter, we are
warned that a fearsome "four horns" will one day appear on the scene,
wreaking havoc against nations lined up to remove the land from Israel.
Therefore, the appearance of these "four horns" will mark the unfolding
of an important biblical time and will represent a significant prophetic
fulfillment and a sign to those living during its day.[15] Here is the case that
it has begun. First, look at the Scripture.

> Then lifted I up my eyes, and saw, and behold four **horns**. And
> I said unto the angel that talked to me, What be these? And he
> answered me, These are the **horns** which have scattered Judah,
> Israel, and Jerusalem. And the LORD shewed me four carpen-
> ters. Then said I, What come these to do? And he spake, say-
> ing, These are the **horns** which have scattered Judah, so that no
> man did lift up his head: but these are come to fray them, to
> cast out the **horns** of the Gentiles, which lifted up their **horn**
> over the land of Judah to scatter it. Zechariah 1:18-21 KJV
> (Emphasis added).

The Scripture looks for a group of four "horns," or political powers,
that will seek to remove the land from Israel. Notice that these political
powers are repeatedly described in the plural sense as "horns" throughout

the Scripture until the very end of the passage when a shift to the singular takes place describing them as a single "horn." This indicates that these four political powers will be separate entities, therefore they are "four horns," but will ultimately come together to act as one "horn" to remove the land. Now notice something else.

This passage is not called the "four nations" prophecy, but the "four horns," and the difference is significant. Had the word "nations" been used, then this group would have been limited to exactly that, actual nation states. But, instead, "horns" was used, which represents a broader political power and can include a nation state, as well as a host of other political powers including organizations that include a multitude of nations. Now consider something else within the Scripture.

The prophecy indicates that two things will happen relative to these "four horns." First, they will be dedicated to scattering the land. And secondly, those efforts will result in a fraying against them after Divine "carpenters" are sent. So let's look at what has been happening since April 30, 2003.

It was on that date that the newly formed international group referred to as the Quartet, consisting of the United States, Russia, the United Nations, and the European Union introduced for the first time their "Road Map for Peace" plan, which had a single purpose. The ultimate goal of this group of four political powers was to remove the restored land of Israel in the name of "peace." Notice that of the Quartet's four participants, two are nation states, and the other two are an organization of nation states. Thus, only the prophetic word "horn" perfectly describes them. This should be a problem for those who attempt to place the "four horns" as nations in Israel's distant past, because if that were the case, then the word "nations" would have been a better prophetic fit than the broader term "horns."[16]

However, on the same date that the Quartet met, what weather experts describe as the "worst weather in U.S. history" began a four-week rampage that included 562 tornadoes and over 1,500 hail storms. Then not long after it ended, across the Atlantic in Europe, the other main participant in the Quartet, the European Union, experienced the worst heat wave in over 250 years. After it had finally ended, a staggering 50,000 lives had been lost.[17] Such an event with its timing certainly qualifies for a fulfillment of the prophetic warning.

But the Quartet made another significant move against the land. In November 2007, they would succeed in gathering 67 nations and nation-state organizations from across the globe to a "peace" conference in Annapolis, Maryland, dedicated to scattering the restored lands from Israel. Although they met in November 2007, the launching of the effort can be traced to the week of July 23, 2007, when the Quartet's point man, former British Prime Minister Tony Blair, began his first trip to the Middle East to promote the Annapolis Conference. Ironically, the subtle beginning of what would become known as the Global Financial Meltdown began within a day of his arrival, as documented in detail within *The Israel Omen*.[18] But there is more to support the contention that this group of four dedicated to scattering the land is the Quartet.

Also of note is the fact that at no time in Israel's past has a group of four gathered for the purpose of removing the land. And since the prophecy goes from the plural to the singular, indicating they would so act together, this creates a problem for those claiming its fulfillment took place long ago. Another case made by those claiming that this prophecy was fulfilled in the past is that the reason Zechariah did not specifically name the "four horns" was because everyone inherently already knew who they were when the prophecy was written. But what refutes that logic is that throughout his book, he names many different cities, nations, and regions. Since he shows no aversion to doing so throughout his book, then logically, it infers he would have done so here as well. Since he did not, then this infers he could not, and the most likely reason is that three participants of the "four horns" had not yet come into existence.

Those claiming that this prophecy was fulfilled in the past typically list the following nations as the ones that Zechariah was referring to: Rome, Babylon, Greece, and Persia. But there is a major problem with this. Although both Rome and Babylon did scatter the Jews, Greece did not, and Persia actually restored them, so it does not complete the prophecy.

It appears that this biblical entity, Zechariah's "four horns," has arrived, adding its weight to the significance of the current times. And with the "coincidences" of disasters to efforts at removing the biblical Promised Land, the focal point appears to be on Israel. Considering all of this, if the events on September 11, 2001, also fulfilled the Isaiah 9 warning, then America is clearly in the mix as well.

Adding weight to it all have been signs in the heavens that have shown like bright billboards, marking the unfolding of great events relative to the Jews, and then Israel, after it was back in the land. These "billboards," seldom erected high in the heavens over the last 2,000 years, have been occurring with a marked new frequency since the 1948 rebirth of the Jewish state.[19] And with these heavenly signs coinciding with big events relating to Israel, and the unfolding of ancient biblical prophecies concerning it all, other unusual events have been stirring across the world as well.

The resignation of a Pope is a big deal, if for no other reason than it almost never happened in an institution that has been around a very long time, the Catholic Church. Individuals who reach the exalted position of pontiff immediately reach the status as the world's most recognizable religious figure. So when Pope Benedict announced on February 21, 2013, that he was resigning from the Papacy, it sent shock waves from one end of the religious world to the other.[20] And, ironically, before this great religious event on Earth, only three days earlier was the great heavenly event in Russia: a large asteroid burning through its sky the likes of which nobody alive can remember ever seeing.[21] Perhaps, it was just a heavenly coincidence to the Earthly event, but there was another wrinkle to it all as well.

The focal point of the Catholic Church worldwide is the Vatican, its seat of power nestled within the city of Rome. And within the Vatican is the best-known western religious structure in the world, Saint Peter's Basilica. Its history began in the year 322 A.D., taking about 30 years to build. It has been the site of grand coronations such as the one for Charlemagne, who is credited with stopping the Muslim masses from conquering all of Europe. That original structure was completely rebuilt in the 1500s with its image, eventually, becoming inexorably linked in the minds of most people to the power of the papacy.[22] But on the day that Pope Benedict resigned, another astronomically rare event coincided with that rare religious one.

A French news crew in town to hear what the Pope was going to say during his scheduled talk had noticed after his stunning and surprising announcement that the weather had suddenly turned bad. Thinking there might be a chance of Saint Peter's Basilica being struck by lightning, they set up their camera and waited. Ironically, lightning struck it with the incredulous camera crew unprepared to take the photo at that moment. But as if it was meant to be captured on film for posterity to gaze upon, about ten seconds later, lightning struck the same spot with the image, that time, captured.[23] It had struck the pinnacle of Saint Peter's Basilica twice, something old sayings tell us should never happen. Perhaps it is nothing but odd coincidence, but it is strange that such a celestial event would occur within a couple of hours of the resignation of a world religious leader, the likes of which had not been seen in almost 600 years.

Whether or not Benedict's resignation and the rise of the new Pope to power will be an event of significance only the future will tell. But one thing is certain the heavens have been active around this big religious event.

Another event has unfolded in recent years and appears to be so unlikely as to be odd. That is the rise of Barack Obama from utter obscurity into the most powerful seat of power in the world, and if it is anything, it is very strange to the point of eerie. In fact, even Mr. Obama has acknowledged his "spooky good fortune" in politics, as noted in a 2008 article in *The New York Times*. It is as though the path to the presidency was cleared every step of the way. And then, once in the exalted position, his reelection was guaranteed by the most unlikely events unfolding to his benefit.

CHAPTER THREE

The Rise of Barack Obama

The rise of Barack Obama to the United States presidency was as unlikely as it was amazing. From the obscurity of a non-accomplished state Senator, to the most powerful political/military position in the world, and it all happened within a four-year time frame.[1] Suddenly, this man from nowhere was placed in a position to transform America into the image of his beliefs. But it's not just America he can change as president, but the Middle East as well. And he appears well on his way to accomplishing both. All of this has occurred in spite of his having associated with numerous radical individuals, any one of whom could have ended the presidential aspirations of any other politician. But in the case of Barack Obama, the media would suddenly become uninterested in such things. Consider his amazing rise to power and the incredible good fortune that surrounds it.

THE COMING MIDEAST WAR AND PEACE TREATY

* * * * *

It was election night in Illinois and as the votes were being counted across the state, candidates running for the State Senate and House of Representatives eagerly awaited the result from months of campaigning. But in the city of Chicago, Senate seat number 9 to be exact, there were no votes to be counted, and it wasn't because the incumbent ran unopposed and simply waltzed back into office. Amazingly, a newcomer had just picked off the coveted seat without opposition. As the State Senator-elect strode to the podium to deliver his victory speech, there was no mention of any concession calls from defeated foes seeking to immediately curry his favor. This strange setting was simply because this newcomer had experienced the most unlikely kind of victory.

As the year 1996 came roaring in, so too approached the Chicago election cycle, and along with it, candidates seeking to become the next State Senator, State Representative, or Ward Committeeman. The real plum in it all was the State Senate seats, positions from which statewide political careers could be launched. And for State Senate seat number 9, located in the heart of Chicago, the incumbent, Alice Palmer, would be challenged by four hopefuls. One of those was an attorney from Chicago's Kenwood neighborhood by the name of Barack Obama.[2] However, a strange thing happened on the way to election night.

In order to qualify as a candidate for an Illinois State Senate seat, there is a requirement that the candidate acquire the signatures of at least 750 voters within their district on a petition favoring their candidacy. Such a requirement is, ostensibly, done to weed out individuals from placing their names on the ballot who are not really serious, allowing the voters to choose from "real" candidates only. Therefore, in accordance with that requirement, all of the candidates for Senate 9 complied with the mandate, submitting their petitions to the Chicago Board of Elections. However, fully aware of how Chicago politics can work, each gathered many more names and signatures than the law required. Palmer, the incumbent in the race, submitted 1,580 signatures on her petition, more than double what was required to ensure that her name would appear for reelection. Gha-is-F. Askia, a challenger for the seat, submitted a whopping 1,899 names on her petition. The remaining two candidates submitted 1,286 and 1,100 signatures, still substantially more than the 750 needed.[3]

The reason why each submitted so many more than the required 750 was to allow for a margin of error in case somebody challenged the validity of any of the signatures they had gathered. In the event of a challenge, the overkill would protect their candidacy from being stillborn by their names being kept off the ballot. And it was a good thing each did this because somebody did challenge the petitions of all candidates seeking State Senate seat number 9, including the incumbent's, except for one. The only candidate not challenged was the one from Kenwood, Barack Obama.

The challenger to their petitions, one Ron Davis, would bring them all before the Chicago Board of Elections (CBOE), contending that each of their petitions represented massive fraud and should be thrown out. However, in addition to the challenge of those four petitions for the senate 9 seat, there would also be challenges to the petitions of candidates running for other offices—a total of ten others, in fact. They too would be brought before the CBOE. But for some strange reason the results from those ten challenges would be dramatically different from those for senate 9. Of those ten, when the dust cleared, only one would be disqualified, based on not having enough signatures. Within the petitions of those ten challenges, the Chicago Board would find an average of 36% of the signatures had to be thrown out. Although it was a high percentage of the overall signatures on the petitions, because those candidates had supplied substantially more signatures than were required by law, all but one candidate would be allowed on their respective ballot. So, only one out of those ten challenged was disqualified, representing a rate of 10%, with the average percent of petition signatures disqualified at 36%. Essentially, the impact of the challenges to those ten petitions was minor. However, for some reason the results for Senate seat number 9 would be dramatically different.[4]

Of the 1,899 signatures submitted by Gha-is F. Askia, the Board found 1,211 to be invalid, or 64%, causing her petition to contain only 688 valid names, 62 short of the required 750, resulting in her name not being allowed on the ballot. The incumbent, Alice Palmer, would experience 1,023 of the 1,580 signatures she submitted being rejected, a dismissal rate of 65%, resulting in those allowed to be counted to be only 557, or 193 short. Ironically, even though she was the incumbent running for reelection, her name would not appear on the ballot. The remaining two candidates would experience a 70%, and 48% rate of signature dismissals, resulting in both being disqualified from having their names on the ballot. This resulted in an average rate of disqualification of 62% without one candidate being allowed to place their name on the ballot, or a 100% disqualification rate.[5] As a result of this strange anomaly to the qualifying process, attorney Barack Obama became the State Senator-elect for seat number 9 without even having to run a race. Although highly beneficial to Mr. Obama, the impact on the other four people was probably not small.

Typically, when individuals go about gathering signatures to be on a ballot, they end up with a sizable investment in the effort, both in terms of money as well as an emotional commitment. And their effort to gather so many more names than required shows the extent of how important it was to them. There is little doubt that those individuals viewed their being kept off the ballot as a great misfortune that befell them. But they were not the only ones to experience misfortune from what transpired.

Thousands of voters in the district also suffered from the unpleasant experience of having a new state senator chosen for them by default. In fact, those who liked their incumbent Senator could not even vote to reelect her. No doubt that had to leave many in the district disturbed and dismayed that a misfortune befell them in that manner.

But that amazingly good fortune of State Senator-elect Obama would only be the beginning of what would become an unending string of the best political luck imaginable. So much so, that in the ensuing years, numerous political reporters, including syndicated columnist Charles Krauthammer, would acknowledge what many others are beginning to realize: Barack Obama is the luckiest politician alive.

*   *   *   *   *

We see it every election cycle. The Democrats offer a well-funded candidate for an open U.S. Senate seat and the Republicans do the same. Then in addition to the two main contenders seeking the prestigious office, there usually appear a number of minor candidates whose combined vote will represent a small percent of the overall votes cast. Those minor candidates have little or no money and even less name recognition. The pattern is so consistent that it's hardly even noticed any longer. However, an unusual exception to this happened in the 2004 U.S. Senate race in Illinois. In this case the exception occurred when a State Senator by the name of Barack Obama, severely underfunded and unknown, became a candidate for that office.

When he entered the race, the Democrats already had a strong, well-funded, and well-known candidate running in their primary by the name of Blair Hull. And as such, they were fairly well united behind him. So, essentially, Hull would have to get past the unknown and grossly underfunded Barack Obama to be the party's standard bearer in the general election. As is typical in such contests, it would take a miracle for Obama to win the primary against him. And if somehow he did win, then he would need good fortune to smile on him again in the general election against the well-funded and also well-known Republican, Jack Ryan. Amazingly, he would get both of those miracles.[6] This according to the Free Republic:

> Did not Clarence Page's own Chicago Tribune and local Chicago newsman Chuck Goudie give unusually heavy coverage of the divorce records of Democrat Blair Hull and Republican Jack Ryan to the benefit of previously invisible, underfunded, candidate with the slenderest of legislative records, named Barack Obama? Was it accidental or a coincidence that the two opponents with the financial resources to bury Mr. Obama in the primary or general elections were relentlessly hammered on "scandals" by the Trib while the same paper ran multipage "puff" pieces on Saint Obama.[7]

Indeed, both powerful candidates were hammered relentlessly by major Illinois media, with the previously invisible Barack Obama benefiting from "multipage puff" pieces written about him. After a period of time, the telling effects of the unusual media combination began to show.

Eventually, as media pressure built on both Hull and Ryan, each withdrew from the race and Mr. Obama went on to win the United States Senate seat against the extremely weak Republican candidate who appeared to have little chance from the start, having moved to Illinois in order to make the race. But as for the supporters and contributors who had invested in Mr. Hull and Mr. Ryan's campaigns, their respective withdrawals and scandals would cut to the quick.[8] Both were large campaigns with lots of people involved. And as their dreams of winning a U.S. senate seat were ending, so too ended the right of voters in Illinois from having a real choice in the race. As such, once again Mr. Obama waltzed into higher public office. Now here is a challenge. Try to find another example of such good political fortune. Good luck, it won't be easy.

*   *   *   *   *

There is a great political benefit derived from being named the keynote speaker for a national political convention. It provides nationwide exposure, as well as a platform for those harboring national ambition. As such, it is coveted by the most powerful politicians in the nation. In 1984, the well-established New York Governor, Mario Cuomo, received the call. He was a major rising star in the Democratic Party. Then in 1988, the political plum went to then, Texas Governor, Ann Richards, another big name Democrat. In 1992, it was Georgia firebrand, Governor Zell Miller. He was a big southern name at the time Bill Clinton was seeking to consolidate the South. In 1996, it went to the popular governor of Indiana, Evan Bayh. He had established his credentials within the party and was a potential candidate for the presidency in 2000.[9] In that year the party's actual nominee, Al Gore, handpicked his fellow Tennessean, U.S. Representative Harold Ford to deliver it. And, indeed, such powerful and established rising stars in the party would be called upon to deliver the speech time and again. However, at the 2004 Democratic convention, the keynote speaker was not an established national name, but a state senator from Illinois whose distinction was that he was a candidate for the U.S. Senate.[10] His name was Barack Obama. How odd, but certainly beneficial to him. So beneficial did it prove to his political career, that he was able to begin running for president just two years later. So after only two years since he had been a state senator with the "slenderest of legislative records," he became a candidate for the U.S. presidency.

*   *   *   *   *

Then after instantly rising as a major candidate in the race for the Democratic nomination in 2008, he managed to defeat heavily favored Hillary Clinton and the legendary Clinton national political machine.

THE COMING MIDEAST WAR AND PEACE TREATY

His campaign was brilliantly run, its theme of "Change" exactly what the Bush-weary electorate wanted to hear. But in the general election, it started to become a different story. After the choice of Sarah Palin for Vice President by the Republican candidate, John McCain, national polls about seven weeks out from the election showed McCain with a slight lead over the unknown Obama. One of the reasons appeared to be the electorate's discomfort with how little they knew about him, not long out of being an obscure state legislator. After all, the media appeared incredibly uninterested in his past, and just as in his Illinois senate race, every media report about him appeared to be a "puff" piece.

Down in the polls, his amazing streak of good fortune appeared to have finally come to an end. He had won a U.S. Senate seat under the most unlikely of circumstances. He had been the unlikely choice for keynote speaker four years earlier, propelling the then state senator to national attention. His fawning media allies helped him overcome the Clinton political machine. But now things began to get a little dicey. He had risen rapidly to the highest political levels through a string of good fortune. But all that seemed to be coming to an end. And then fate appeared again by his side.

About seven weeks before the election, an event that had not happened since 1929 began unfolding.[11] Financial institutions that were the bedrock of the American banking system began to collapse in rapid succession, with the Bush Administration taking the brunt of the blame. What precipitated the suddenness of it was unusual. The Bush Administration had been bailing out multiple financial institutions over the course of the previous year to keep the nation's system from cascading into a total meltdown. But then, and completely out of line with their previous approach, they refused to bail out the investment giant Lehman Brothers. This sudden shift in approach took place only six weeks before the 2008 presidential election.[12]

The reason Bush Administration officials had been dedicated to bailing out those reckless institutions was because the whole system had become so interconnected, creating the potential of giant financial dominos toppling one after the other. But for some strange reason they chose not to bail out Lehman Brothers, and the results were twofold and immediate. First, those feared financial dominos did begin coming down, just as had been feared, precipitating the worst crisis since the Great Depression and causing panic among an electorate that was preparing to elect a new president.[13] Secondly, the fear that resulted guaranteed the election of unknown Barack Obama to the presidency. From the moment the crisis broke, the electorate appeared to no longer care about how little they knew about him, preferring "change" without much thought given to its direction. Thereafter, he pulled ahead of McCain, never to look back. Exactly why the Bush Administration decided to suddenly change its approach to dealing with those weak financial institutions at that precise moment is not known. But what is known is the ultimate impact it had on the election going on at that time. And across the world, the devastating impact of the financial meltdown on the lives of countless people would reverberate for years to come.

Throughout the election Mr. Obama would avoid questions about his association with the most questionable types of characters, past and even current associates, any one of which could bring down the national potential of any politician. But he would walk through it all completely unquestioned, and as a result, his campaign was, amazingly, unfazed by such threats. Such characters would include William Ayres and his wife, Bernadine Dorn, former members of the Weather Underground, America's first terrorist group, which bombed the Pentagon in the 1960s. There would be enough connections between the two former terrorists and Mr. Obama to keep several journalists busy for a long time. But strangely, none would question Obama's career-killing relationship.[14]

THE COMING MIDEAST WAR AND PEACE TREATY

Although the Communist Party in the United States is a speck on the map, somehow Mr. Obama would find a way to locate it in a person whom he would acknowledge in his book, Dreams of My Father, as his mentor, Frank Marshall Davis. And this relationship too, would go undisclosed to the public during the campaign. Even his pastor, the virulently anti-America Jeremiah Wright would not impact him, the mainstream media leaving the public unaware of the strong relationship there, with Obama once again able to escape career-killing coverage of it.[15] The list of such characters would go on and on. Anita Dunn, eventually to become White House Communication Director, would openly avow the late Chinese Communist leader, Mao Zedong, as someone whose political writings were a guide for her. The problem in mentioning him was that in the warlike 20th century, Mao historically fits best with such infamous characters as Adolf Hitler and Joseph Stalin, all mass murderers. Unimaginably, no harm would befall Barack Obama from his relationship with her as well. And the reason why was simple: the mass media would, strangely, ignore such hot stories one after another granting a pass of historical proportions to the unknown Obama.

* * * * *

One must realize that in the 2012 presidential election, three separate and unpredictable events unfolded with two being storms and one a computer system called Project Orca. For starters, let's look at the storms. Conventions are designed to be a grand send-off for their presidential candidates. They are designed to showcase individuals and ideas with an eye on the future. And the 2012 convention cycle was no different. Except this time an unpredictable event occurred that placed the Republicans at a distinct disadvantage. As the Republican Convention was being held in Tampa, Hurricane Isaac took aim at the city. The timing was terrible, causing one of its four precious days of intense national exposure to be lost, and shifting the national focus from the convention message to the storm. Additionally, its keynote speaker, the Hispanic Florida Senator Marco Rubio, was moved from prime time.[16] This was a significant blow because he was aiming to secure the Hispanic vote for the Republican nominee Mitt Romney.

However, in spite of the shaky sendoff the Republican candidate began to catch up with the president on the shoulders of a debate performance that served as a catapult for his campaign. And as the race entered the final week, the most reliable polls indicated Mr. Romney and Mr. Obama in a very tight race but with Mr. Romney slightly ahead and with momentum. Then, incredibly, fate appeared to inject itself again. A new storm, the likes of which caused it to be referred to as another "Perfect Storm," suddenly struck the Northeast coast. What Hurricane Sandy did was freeze the clear momentum of Mr. Romney dead in its tracks, allowing the president to regain his campaign footing and stop his political bleeding. This from *The New York Times* polling guru Nate Silver just before the votes were counted ...

> If President Obama wins re-election on Tuesday, the historical memory of the race might turn on the role played by Hurricane Sandy. Already, some analysts are describing the storm as an "October surprise" that allowed Mr. Obama to regain his footing after stumbling badly in the first presidential debate and struggling to get back on course. Some Republicans seem prepared to blame a potential defeat for Mitt Romney on the storm, and the embrace of Mr. Obama by New Jersey Gov. Chris Christie and other public officials.[17]

Indeed, not only did the storm stop the Romney campaign's momentum dead in its tracks, but it also provided the president the opportunity to have the focus taken off of election issues that were hurting him, and place it on the need to assist those whom the terrible misfortune befell, impacted by the highly unusual weather event. In addition to that incredibly beneficial turn of events for Mr. Obama, a nationally popular Republican governor of one of the states hardest hit, New Jersey, was seen embracing the president as he made a presidential visit to the state. And a picture is worth a thousand words. It gave the temporary appearance that the president was one who could work with Republicans, even though his first term was marked by strong partisanship. But as helpful as the oddball storm was, fate wasn't finished yet. With the race still close, the winner would now be decided by which campaign did the best job of getting out its vote.

The Romney campaign had invested over $40 million in a computer system designed to do exactly that. And on the day of the election, there were over 30,000 volunteers ready to reap the benefits of voters identified as favorable to their candidate in the previous months. Millions of those voters phone numbers were stored within this vast computer system, which was called Project Orca. Then fate injected itself again. In an article after the election titled, "Insiders Explain How Mitt Romney's Campaign Completely Fell Apart On Election Day," Business Insider looked at Project Orca's complete collapse.[18] Project Orca experienced a major failure on the day of the election. As a result, the 30,000+ volunteers, ready to call millions of voters identified as supporting their man, were unable to reach the multitudes because the system was unable to retrieve the millions of voters and their phone numbers so a volunteer could call them. As a result, some percentage of the Romney vote did not turn out.[19] With the combination of significant misfortunes, well-timed storms, along with the collapse of Project Orca, the incredible luck of Barack Obama secured him reelection.

*   *   *   *   *

Having secured the most powerful office in the world after a meteoric rise from obscurity, the reelection of President Obama to a second term, strangely, appeared to also be touched by the hand of fate. And the entire litany of incredible luck and lack of scrutiny all begs the same question: What is it all leading to? Is there some action that fate has set aside for him to accomplish?

There is something else associated with each of these fortuitous events that propelled Barack Obama into the presidency, and this common denominator may offend some. Consider the litany from another perspective.

When he ran for the state senate seat, misfortune came the way of the four others seeking to fulfill their dreams of service to the people of that district, one of whom was the incumbent. There is no telling how much of their personal funds and time was already spent by the time they were disqualified. And there were probably other negative impacts on their lives going forward from suffering the stigma of not even being able to qualify to run for public office after making a big show of it all. Additionally, the citizens in that district experienced misfortune by being prevented from exercising their right of choosing their representative. Instead, essentially, one was chosen for them by default.

When he ran for the U.S. Senate, it was again the misfortune of others that played out uniquely in his favor, allowing him to win the coveted position with little opposition. In this case the misfortune struck the two favorites in the race and was especially personal and, no doubt, painful. Here too the electorate would share in that misfortune by not really having a choice in the election.

When he ran for the presidency in 2008, his campaign would be a juggernaut in the Democratic primaries, overcoming the powerful Clinton machine and going on to take the nomination. However, in the general election it would be a different matter. About six weeks out from the election, Senator John McCain would be leading, with Obama appearing to have stalled. But suddenly, all of that changed with the global financial meltdown. That misfortune which took place on a global scale propelled Senator Barack Obama past McCain and into the White House.

When running for reelection, the president had a lot of handicaps. The economy was still down, and his opponent was well-funded. And as the election headed into the finish line, Mr. Romney appeared to be slightly ahead of Mr. Obama in the polls. However, Hurricane Sandy, which brought great misfortune to many people who were struck by it, completely ended Mr. Romney's momentum, greatly aiding the president in getting reelected. An additional misfortune struck on the day of the election, and it was focused on Mr. Romany in the complete collapse of his $40 million get-out-the-vote computer system. Both misfortunes contributed heavily to the president's reelection win.

There is one overriding common denominator associated with the rise of Barack Obama: the misfortune of others. Literally, without misfortune befalling a litany of other people, his political career would have been stillborn long ago. Although such an observation is one many would prefer not to acknowledge, it is also undeniably the common denominator that if removed alters everything. Would he have won that state senate race had the incumbent and three other challengers been running? Would he have overcome powerful candidates, one a Democrat, and the other a Republican, seeking that Illinois U.S. Senate seat? It is difficult to argue that he would have won either race. And both were critical to launching his career. Would he have defeated John McCain for the presidency had the global financial meltdown not happened exactly when it did? It is possible, but maybe not. Would he have won reelection to the presidency had Hurricane Sandy not struck when it did, and project Orca collapsed? It is possible, but maybe not.

CHAPTER FOUR

Israel Surrounded

T he Middle East expansion of the British Empire after the First World War came at the expense of the Ottoman Empire, whose unfortunate fate had been to side with Germany in that war.[1] And along with their defeat had departed the land known as Palestine, also known as the Holy Land where once had existed the nation of Israel, and kings like David and Solomon. But it wouldn't take long before the new rulers of the ancient land, would realize what the Romans many years before them had: it was also almost ungovernable, consisting of "unreasonable" people. As a result, after the conclusion of the Second World War the mighty British lion turned Palestine over to the newly formed United Nations to dispose of in whatever manor it saw fit.[2]

On September 29, 1947, the U.N. would decide to divide it between the Arabs and Jews living in the area, into two new states, one Jewish and the other Arab, drawing the borders according to the density of their populations in the region. But instead of opting for their state, the Palestinian Arabs would choose to join a host of Arab nations that swore to pounce on the vastly outnumbered Jews the moment they dared to declare their independence. And true to their word on May 15, 1948, the day after Israel declared its independence, the attacks began.[3]

Israel would win her war for independence, but in spite of that amazing victory, her neighbors would refuse to accept her existence.[4] Over the course of time Israel would have to fight more wars against those that promised to drive her into the sea. But of the four hostile nations on her borders: Syria, Lebanon, Jordan, and Egypt, it was Egypt that really counted. Egypt's population was several times greater than the combined populations of the other three nations and was also able to field an army that was a major threat. Without Egypt, the coalition of nations against the Jews would crumble. And in September 1978, that is exactly what happened.

After having lost the vast Sinai desert to Israel in the 1967 war, the Egyptians finally decided their interests were best served by signing a peace treaty with the Jewish State in return for that land. And with the signing of the historical Camp David Peace Accord, suddenly the strategic picture of threats against Israel was radically altered.[5] With the loss of Egypt from the Arab coalition, and with Jordan quietly making peace as well, Israel was secure. Although she would continue to experience an array of minor wars on her borders with Lebanon and Syria, the constant threat of another major war had come to an end. That strategic picture would remain the same throughout the 1980s and into the new millennium. However, coinciding with the election of Barack Obama to the United States presidency, things would begin to change.

In *The Israel Omen II*, there are three chapters dedicated to what appears to have unfolded behind the scenes within the Obama Administration as it pertains to Israel. Although some have criticized it as being overly critical of the president, it has been confirmed by unfolding events.

And just for the record, both *The Israel Omen* and *The Israel Omen II* were critical of the previous three presidents as well. During his first term President Obama changed U.S. policy toward Israel in the clear direction to what the Palestinian side wants. And this has been done without much regard for the security of Israel.[6] Yes, Israel has received great amounts of military hardware from the U.S., but those weapons cannot offset the loss of security that will result from the loss of lands the president seeks to remove in the name of peace. He has pushed aside assurances from previous presidents given to Israel to extract concessions from her in order to enact his plan. No doubt, this has to be quite disturbing to the leadership of tiny Israel, not knowing what U.S. commitment will fall next. The president did not visit Israel in his first term, but instead went early to Egypt, and, shockingly, gave an initial nod of approval to the out-lawed Muslim Brotherhood, which eventually took over there. That nod came in the form of an invitation sent to their leadership to attend his big Cairo speech, his first made overseas, marking it as very important. The invitation would be a slap in the face to America's ally, Egyptian President Hosni Mubarak, and send a message to Islamists across the Middle East that would not be missed.[8]

It is this same Muslim Brotherhood, as noted by Caroline Glick writing in the *Jerusalem Post*, who during the November 2012 flare-up in Gaza experienced a "stormy meeting" relating to what to do about the Israeli incursion into that terrorist enclave. The incursion represented an effort to put a stop to the repeated rocket attacks into Israel from Gaza. The debate within the ranks of the Brotherhood in Egypt centered on whether or not to make war on Israel immediately, or wait until the Egyptian military was better prepared. After much heated debate, those in favor of more military preparation prevailed. There was then a cease-fire stopping the Israeli military action, an effort intended to secure a rocket-free future for Israeli families near the Gaza border. But the cease-fire, supported by the Obama Administration, actually placed the radical Muslim Brotherhood in a position of power broker between Israel and Hamas. Yet Hamas, an offshoot of the Muslim Brotherhood, is a dedicated terrorist organization.

Since it was brokered by Egypt's President Morsi, of the Muslim Brotherhood, the same one seeking Israel's destruction, it has granted his increasingly repressive regime a form of legitimacy in the "peace" process that is completely unwarranted. And it places Israel on the same moral plane as Hamas. This is how Glick puts it.

> At best, Israel and Hamas are placed on the same moral plane. The cease-fire erases the distinction between Israel, a peace-seeking liberal democracy that simply wants to defend its citizens, and Hamas, a genocidal jihadist terrorist outfit that seeks the eradication of the Jewish people and the destruction of Israel.[8]

And even worse, as Glick notes...

> Moreover, Obama and Clinton compelled Israel to accept wording in the cease-fire that arguably makes Egypt the arbiter of Israeli and Palestinian compliance with the agreement.[9]

It is not difficult to understand that the act of placing one's enemy over you, in any form, is a tacit alliance with them against you. In this case the enemy is one that had, until only recently, been ruled by a dictator friendly to peace with Israel. Apparently not understanding the consequences of their actions, it was President Obama and his Secretary of State, Hillary Clinton, whose actions early in the administration started a train of events which ultimately replaced the dictatorial American ally, Mubarak, with the increasingly dictatorial Muslim Brotherhood, an enemy of Israel and America.

Effectively, by Obama and Clinton withdrawing support from the long-time American ally Hosni Mubarak in his moment of greatest need, the Muslim Brotherhood was propelled to lead that critical nation on Israel's border. And they are radical to the core. Having been founded in 1928, the Brotherhood aligned with Adolf Hitler in the 1930s and 40s, even translating *Mein Kampf* into Arabic.[10]

Since their consolidation of power, Christians throughout Egypt have suffered persecution that was never a problem under the previous dictator. The Brotherhood's man who became the new president of Egypt, Dr. Morsi, has also grabbed constitutional powers comparable to his predecessor.[11] As ominous as this change in the constellation of powers directly on their border is, something similar began happening to the north of Israel, with the potential to dwarf the new Egyptian threat.

Reviving the Caliphate

After the breakup of the old Ottoman Empire following the First World War, the Muslims of the Middle East have existed in a fractured state characterized by various nation states frequently at odds with one another. Such a condition has prevented it from acting as one giant Muslim nation, or, caliphate. To understand what a caliphate is, here is a partial definition of it from the *Encyclopedia Britannica*:

> The political-religious state comprising the Muslim community and the lands and peoples under its dominion ...

It was the united nature of the Middle East under the Ottoman Empire that allowed it to become a major factor in the First World War, siding with Germany in that conflict, which ultimately led to its breakup. But for Muslims across the Middle East and the world, the restoration of this caliphate is of the utmost importance. And since Egypt has been turned over to the Muslim Brotherhood, excitement has been growing within their ranks that this dream is unfolding. Many of its members in positions of authority openly speak about it. One such individual, Brotherhood Cleric, Safwat Higazi, before thousands of supporters gathered in Egypt would excitedly announce:

> We can see how the dream of the Islamic caliphate is being realized, God willing, by Dr. Mohamed Mursi … The capital of the caliphate—-the capital of the United States of the Arabs—-will be Jerusalem, God willing… Our capital will not be Cairo, Mecca or Medina"[12]

Dr. Morsi, of course, is the current Muslim Brotherhood leader of Egypt, having replaced the Israel/American friendly Mubarak. Within the new Egyptian constitution, written by the Brotherhood, it spells out for any willing to look what its ultimate goal is, stating that the constitution "prepares the way for an Islamic caliphate." And that is where the nation of Turkey comes into play.

The remnant of the late Ottoman Empire is the nation of Turkey, which is strategically located between the Middle East and Europe. With the breakup of their empire after the First World War, Turkey became a secular state under the leadership of Kemal Ataturk. In his efforts to move Turkey toward the west, he would ban the Islamic fez hat for men and the headscarf for women from being worn in public. He also realized that Islamist fanatics would forever seek to regain power, never willing to accept anything but Islamist rule for the nation. So committed was Ataturk to keeping Turkey from falling under the control of religious zealots, that he established a system wherein they would be prevented from doing so even long after his death. He placed the ultimate responsibility of keeping Turkey a secular state in the hands of the military, authorizing it to take power away from any regime that began to turn the nation into an Islamist state. And thus, since 1924 when this system was put in place, Turkey remained a secular society kept out of the hands of Islamists.[14]

As such, it was Turkey, a powerful and populous country to the north of Israel that formed a kind of alliance with the Jewish state. Not being an Islamist state, that was acceptable for them to do. Each in the relationship benefited, but Israel more because Turkey helped alleviate their isolated status within the neighborhood called the Middle East. Like the neutralizing of Egypt from the Camp David Peace Accords, the "alliance" with Turkey not only neutralized another huge Muslim country, but even provided a rare alliance for the Jews. However, although Turkey was a secular state since 1924 and an ally of Israel's for many years, in the year 2009, all of that began to change.

It would be under the new Obama Administration that the move taking Turkey in an Islamist direction really got going. The President of Turkey, Abdullah Gul, succeeded in passing legislation that allowed military personnel "threatening national security" to be tried in a civilian court, virtually guaranteeing the end of their role since the days of Ataturk in preventing the rise of an Islamist regime in the country. Then in 2010, with their new-found power, a civilian court would purge military ranks beginning with 70 top officers arrested on "conspiracy" charges. By 2011, the president of Turkey would appoint a host of top military officers after their predecessors resigned en masse—-300, in fact.[14] And with these actions for the first time since 1924, a civilian government decided who ran the military, a guarantee of the end of Turkey as a secular state. And as the move toward becoming an Islamist state picked up steam, so, too, did efforts to break the alliance with Israel. In fact, such a move against the Jews is in perfect harmony with Islamist theology.

The break would come during Israel's sea and land blockade of Gaza, which was an attempt to prevent rockets from reaching the Muslim Brotherhood offshoot, Hamas, which governed the area. In line with Brotherhood orthodoxy, those rockets would, invariably, find their way into Israeli towns located near the border with Gaza. The simple goal of Hamas for firing those rockets into towns is to randomly kill. In spite of the Israeli blockade being established for the protection of its citizens, inexplicably, the Turkish government supported a flotilla of ships destined to break it, in a direct confrontation at sea with Israel. And when the dust settled from the challenge, on the deck of one ship would rest the bodies of nine dead crew members. From this blatant effort to confront Israel, the newly established Islamist Turkish government would break ties with its old ally. Not only did this lead to the end of the military alliance between the two nations, but also to the end of economic and diplomatic cooperation, representing a major shift against Israel.[15]

It is clear from the Prime Minister of Turkey, Recip Erdogan, that it is the goal of the new Turkey to bring back under its wings many of the nations that comprised the old Ottoman Empire, essentially a caliphate. And one necessary step to accomplish this is to shift from being a friend of Israel, to an enemy. In line with that effort, Erdogan would travel to Egypt to bestow a high-level diplomatic visit on the new Islamist government installed there. He would also inflame Arab passions further by stating that "Zionism" is a crime against humanity. And what is "Zionism"?[16] It is the movement of the Jewish people to return to their homeland in the form of their ancient nation Israel. So, essentially, the Turkish leader was indicating that their return as a nation was a crime.

It is noted in various media circles how close President Obama is to the Turkish leader.[17] In line with that, Mr. Obama made it a point to go to Egypt and Turkey while in the Middle East neighborhood, but skipped Israel. Early in his administration the president presented a new condition for talks to begin between Israel and the Palestinians, killing any chance for negotiations in a move that puzzled Middle East observers, including his political allies.[18]

In his big 2011 Middle East speech, President Obama would present draconian terms to the Israelis for peace with the Palestinians.[19] So egregious was this new policy against Israel that about a week prior to the president presenting it, the White House would be forced to announce the resignation of George Mitchell, point man for the U.S. in the Middle East for Obama and the two presidents before him. This was strange in light of the fact that his area of diplomacy had just reached the zenith of world attention.[20] But the message from his resignation was clear, telegraphing to the diplomatic world his intense disapproval of the new harsh anti-Israel policy that was about to be announced. It was a plan that jeopardizes the security of the tiny state by dramatically reducing its borders to the point of being indefensible. Although his resignation letter was announced just a week prior to the president's May 19 speech, it was dated April 6, a full five weeks earlier.[21]

The only logical explanation for the delay was because efforts were being made to persuade him to withdraw it. Had his resignation been announced after the president's speech, then from that would flow the logic that the delay was designed to not disrupt the speech. But it was announced before the president's speech, indicating a high intensity of opposition to the new policy. And there is little doubt that its announcement could have only been at Mitchell's insistence, demonstrating a willingness to displease his president. By releasing it before the president's speech, a signal of disunity within the president's foreign policy team was sent to the world, and that had to be quite disturbing to Obama. Mitchell's obvious insistence on it being released before, indicates the intensity of his opposition to the new policy.

As mentioned earlier, President Obama placed a new condition on Israel for negotiations with the Palestinians to begin on his watch. This new condition came in the form of a construction freeze in East Jerusalem as a precondition for negotiations. It is rare for a moderator to a dispute to add a condition for talks between the parties to begin. And although this action early in his administration was viewed, even by his supporters, as not very competent, he did it again in his May 2011 speech. With the Israeli Prime Minister coming to town to offer some new concession toward the "peace" process in a major speech, the president quickly gave his big speech the day before, cutting Netanyahu to the quick and causing him to not even present his speech nor mention its concessions. One of the president's biggest supporters, Harvard Law Professor Alan Dershowitz, complained that Obama had "hurt the peace process gravely."[22] Understanding these two events leaves us in the uncomfortable position of having to conclude whether the president was incompetent or willful in these acts. But regardless of which you choose, the impact of his actions had the same effect. It has forced the "peace" process to the United Nations, where Israel is hopefully outnumbered.

And then there is the question of Syria. Understandably, President Obama has been cautious with that situation. On the one hand the brutal repression of the Syrian people by the dictator, Bashar al-Assad, repulses all individuals who believe in the basic rights of mankind. But, on the other hand, it is apparent that many of those fighting the Syrian regime are radical Islamists, as reported by *The New York Times*,[23] *USA Today*,[24] and other news outlets. Such a Hobson's choice has led to a lack of any kind of clear policy relating to the mess. But even the existence of that unfortunate circumstance leads to the following question. Would the Syrian uprising have ever happened if the new Obama Administration had not demonstrated a shift toward the Muslim Brotherhood in Egypt, and instead, continued to support the dictator Mubarak? Did not that shift in U.S. policy catch the eye of extremists across the region? And in spite of the horrible nature of the Assad regime, will the people in that nation be better off, in the long run, with an Islamist regime? Considering the results of such regimes in places like Iran, reasonable and compassionate people could easily say no to that question. As bad as the Syrian dictator is, and he *is* bad, he was also no longer a threat to Israel and the peace of the region. It is even reported that he made secret deals with Israel and that his verbal threats against the Jewish state was nothing more than lip service to certain elements within his borders. On the other hand, elements within the Syrian rebels openly talk about Israel being their next target after taking the Syrian capital, Damascus.

There are other actions early in the president's second term that raise more flags of concern. In terms of foreign policy, the two cabinet members that matter the most are the Secretary of State and the Secretary of Defense. Between the two, they address the military and diplomatic side of relations across the globe. And within those positions at the end of his first term was Hillary Clinton and Leon Panetta, respectively, neither one of which possessed any strange or even potentially anti-Israeli views. However, after being safely tucked away in his second term, the president appointed new people to fill those important positions—-individuals who raise questions pertaining to Israel.

His new Secretary of Defense, Chuck Hagel, raises the most serious questions for those concerned about the small Jewish state. The "think tank," Atlantic Council, headed by Hagel, publishes papers pertaining to foreign policy perspectives. In line with that function, it provided one on Israel that likened its possessing the West Bank to that of "Apartheid." Josh Block, a former spokesman for the American Israeli Political Action Committee, would address Hagel's nomination for Secretary of Defense with these words.

> While in the Senate, Hagel voted against designating the Iranian Revolutionary Guard Corps as a terrorist organization, refused to call on the E.U. to designate Hezbollah a terrorist group, and consistently voted against sanctions on Iran for their illicit pursuit of nuclear weapons capability. It is a matter of fact that his record on these issues puts him well outside the mainstream Democratic and Republican consensus.[25]

Zionist Organization of America President, Morton Klein, when first hearing of Hagel's nomination for Defense Secretary by President

Obama stated, "He is one of the most hostile critics of Israel that has ever been in the Senate." Hagel would earn that critique with such actions as being only one of four senators refusing to sign a letter in support of Israel in 2000. In 2004 he also refused to sign a letter urging President Bush to highlight Iran's nuclear program at the G-8 summit. But he did sign a letter to President Obama, in 2009, urging him to indirectly recognize the terrorist organization Hamas by opening negotiations with them.[26] And the litany of complaints against him would go on and on. All of this is not to say every U.S. senator must 100% of the time agree to everything presented in support of Israel. But it is to point out that Hagel is well out of mainstream thinking when it comes to Israeli security. Yet he is now the Secretary of Defense for the United States, placed there by President Obama. But there is something else interesting to all of this.

Before Leon Panetta, whom Hagel replaced at Defense, there was Robert Gates. Gates was a Bush holdover who served for three years under Obama and decided to retire with one year remaining in the president's first term. President Obama, instead of naming Hagel at that time, convinced Panetta to sign on for a one-year tour of duty at Defense.[27] So the question is raised, why not just nominate Hagel at that time? And the answer appears to be that had the president nominated Hagel then, it would have undermined his Jewish support just as he was entering an election year. In fact, Panetta was moved from the CIA to take the position, retaining it until after the president was safely reelected. Only then did the president reveal that Hagel would join his administration at Defense. If that appears to be a slight of hand designed to avoid issues with his Jewish base, it is because it does appear to be that.

More insight into Hagel's ways of thinking concerning Israel would arrive from a book published in 2008, titled *The Much Too Promised Land*. In it he would be quoted as saying,

I'm not an Israeli senator, I'm a United States senator... I support Israel, but my first interest is I take an oath of office to the
Constitution of the United States, not to a president, not to a
party, not to Israel. If I go run for Senate in Israel, I'll do that.[28]

Few Americans could argue with such sentiments, placing the interest of the United States above those of any other nation. The only problem
with Hagel's remarks is that they present a false choice. Typically, it is almost always in the interest of a nation to be very supportive of their allies,
especially as it concerns Israel, where in the Middle East they are clearly
the only true friend America has. And such support includes times when
the U.S. might be uncomfortable with something being done, but the ally
still needs support even though their actions may not be perfectly in line
with what is wanted. That is because true friendship and alliance should
outweigh any difference on a particular issue and is placed at the center.
Without that kind of an approach, disasters such as the loss of a nation
friendly to the United States occurs, as in the case of Egypt, and years
earlier Iran. Even though both former allies were not perfect, each was
an ally that was later replaced by an enemy. Even worse, Hagel's implicit
inference within such statements implies that those who do steadfastly
stand by the alliance with Israel are somehow disloyal to U.S. interests.

Then there is the State Department, now headed by former Senator
John Kerry. He too would refuse to sign a letter urging sanctions against
Iran for their continued uranium enrichment activities. He would also
adopt the Arab view that Jerusalem is one of "the big three issues" preventing a settlement of the conflict. However, most Israeli supporters see
Jerusalem as the capital of Israel. In line with that reasoning, during the
2012 Democratic convention Kerry ignored the decision of the party
faithful to remove its traditional plank in the convention platform sup-
porting a unified Jerusalem under Israeli control.[29] Then in 2013 after
terrorists detonated bombs at the finish line of the Boston Marathon,

Kerry would equate that with the Israeli actions against ships sent from Turkey to break their blockade meant to prevent the importing of rockets into Gaza.[30] He would do this even though the United Nations commission that was set up to investigate the Gaza incident would rule in favor of Israel's right to enforce the blockade. And it is a rare day when the United Nations sides with Israel. But apparently, on that rare day, Mr. Kerry would not agree.

So with Israel increasingly surrounded by deadly enemies on all sides, this unfortunate state of affairs appears to be related to the rise of President Obama to the U.S. Presidency. And this raises another question. Considering the unusual way he became president, is he a president of fate concerning Israel? Will he be the president that finally achieves the much-coveted "peace" agreement between Israel and the Palestinians?

Some have speculated that since President Obama's father was a Muslim, and having grown up in Indonesia, a Muslim country, that he must secretly be a Muslim too. But there is a problem with this belief. What real Muslim would come out in favor of same-sex marriage? The simple and undeniable answer is none. Therefore, he cannot be a religious-oriented Muslim. But the pattern of his actions relative to the Middle East point to another ideology that, perhaps, fits him better. He appears to promote a form of pan-Arabism that seeks a greater Arab nation across borders, and probably led by his dear friend in Turkey. His strange and highly successful strategy in the Middle East of pushing nations from the friendly or neutral column, to the enemy column relative to America, isolating Israel and other actions, creates legitimate speculation about his core beliefs.

If the president does not embrace Pan-Arabism, then considering the results of his Middle Eastern policies he has, no doubt, pleased those who do. It is true that in the 1970s, under President Jimmy Carter, the strategic nation of Iran went from the pro-western column to the virulently anti-western column, but it was an isolated instance in the Middle East, reflecting a tragic miscalculation. But in the case of President Obama, pro-western and neutral-western Middle Eastern nations are dropping like flies, ultimately to be ruled by Islamists. For those offended by such speculation, the facts should speak for themselves as the region, and the world, will be paying a high price from these developments for a long time to come.

CHAPTER FIVE

Signs in the Heavens

In the beginning of the Bible we are given the details of creation in the Book of Genesis. And therein God laid out the purposes for the heavens to include the division of day and night and for the marking of time. But there is another reason He provides for having created the heavens; so they could be used as "signs" to mankind. Since the world is a big place, where better to post a message than in the heavens? In the first chapter, verse 14 we are told:

> [14]And God said, Let there be lights in the firmament of the heaven to divide the day from the night; and let them be for signs, and for seasons, and for days, and years: Genesis 1:14 KJV[1]

According to Strong's Concordance, the Hebrew translation for the word "signs" is that of a banner, or an omen of some momentous event. The term "seasons" can also indicate an appointed time. Over the course of time, one sign after another would appear in the heavens, like billboards for various generations, erected to alert those in their day who knew what to watch for. And each as it unfolded marked an event of great biblical significance.

It is recorded in the Scriptures that one such celestial event coincided with the birth of Jesus, and even led wealthy wise men traveling great distances to see what the astronomical tumult was all about.[2] Scholars disagree as to the exact date of His birth, but we know from astronomical computer models that in the year 2 B.C., the extremely rare conjunction of Jupiter, known as the King planet, and Venus, known as the Mother planet, came together to produce a star of unusual brightness to the naked eye.[3] But whatever the actual event consisted of, one thing is certain according to the ancient texts, the heavens broadcasted His arrival, and so, too, would they for His death.

Whereas for His birth a light illuminated the arrival of the Light of the World, appropriately, on the day He died, the heavens turned dark. On that day the Scriptures tell us that the sky darkened, and a great earthquake shook the land.[4] From the Book of Matthew we are told, "Now from the sixth hour there was darkness over all the land unto the ninth hour." And here, too, there appears to be a secular record of such an event. This, according to the ancient Greek historian Phlegon:

> In the 4th year of the 202nd Olympiad, there was a great eclipse of the Sun, greater than had ever been known before, for at the sixth hour the day was changed into night, and the stars were seen in the heavens. An earthquake occurred in Bythinia and overthrew a great part of the city of Niceae.[5]

The fourth year of the 202nd Olympiad was in the year 33 A.D. Although much of Phlegon's works would be lost, before they disappeared other authors in his day would quote them. One named Origen, in his book Against Celsus, observed that "Phlegon mentioned the eclipse which took place during the crucifixion of the Lord Jesus and no other."[6]

And other ancient authors as well would use Phlegon's works to further their own writings, indicating how significant his work was viewed by those in his day.

In another account, this one from the ancient author, Tertullian, in his apology to the Rulers of the Roman Empire, that same darkness that fell upon the land is noted.

> In the same hour, too, the light of the day was withdrawn, when the sun at the very time was in his meridian blaze. Those who were not aware that this had been predicted of Christ, no doubt thought it was an eclipse. You yourselves have the account of the world-portent still in your archives.[7]

Both the biblical and historical secular texts agree that the sun ceased providing its light as Jesus suffered on the cross and that this started at the sixth hour, with the biblical text providing when it all ended, the ninth hour.[8] Such a three-hour eclipse of the sun would be the longest in history, since science tells us they normally last only about seven minutes. However, the ancient writings of Phlegon, and a host of others appear to confirm the strange celestial event, calling it a "great eclipse of the sun." So much so that the "day was changed into night," which only the covering of the sun for a great duration could accomplish.[9]

And there is little question that for those who were alive at that time and doubted the Deity of Jesus, the heavens provided an awesome spectacle none could miss. But this kind of event would only benefit those looking and whose minds were open to heavenly "signs." However, although such darkness as never before seen appropriately descended over the land as the "Light of the World" departed it, there would be other heavenly signs that occurred before and after that incredible Jerusalem day.

In the Book of Joel we are told, "The sun shall be turned into darkness, and the moon into blood, before the great and terrible day of the Lord come."[10] And such celestial events involving the moon are referred to as "blood moons," because when a lunar eclipse takes place, for a brief moment it is faintly illuminated with a red light refracted by the Earth's atmosphere, resulting in a red hue on its surface. This refracted hue gives the moon the appearance of being red, and, thus, the term "blood moon."

And it is these "blood moons" where another heavenly announcement marking His death came from, lighting up the heavens for those who knew what to look for. In the Jewish Talmud it is taught that lunar eclipses are a bad omen for Israel, and that a solar eclipse is considered a bad omen for the world.

Almost a year before His crucifixion, on the Jewish Feast Day of Passover, April 14, 32 A.D., a blood moon appeared. It would happen again on the Feast of Tabernacles later that year on October 7, 32 A.D. Although rare for the feast days of Passover and Tabernacles to experience a blood moon in the same year, it repeated again in the following year. On the date April 3, 33 A.D. Passover fell and with it, once again, appeared a blood moon. Then later that year, again coinciding with the Feast of Tabernacles celebrated on September 27, 33 A.D, another blood moon appeared.[11, 12] Such an astronomical phenomenon of four consecutive blood moons falling on Passover and the Feast of Tabernacles, in back-to-back years, is referred to as a "tetrad," and they are not only rare, but viewed as a significant sign in the heavens.[13, 14]

There would be only seven more "tetrads" over the course of the next 1,980 years, starting from the year 33 A.D.[15] However, before the next tetrad arrived, another interesting heavenly sign occurred in the year 70 A.D. In that significant year the Jews observed blood moons on both Passover and the Feast of Tabernacles. Here, too, although not a tetrad, the heavenly sign on those feast days would mark a year of great significance in Jewish history. In that year the holy second Temple of the Jews, built by them after returning from their Babylonian exile, was destroyed by the Roman army. After their defeat at the hands of Rome's legions, a great scattering of their people across the known world began. In that year, blood moons book-ended the destruction of the Temple, which occurred on August 4, 70. The first would appear on Passover, April 14, 70, and the other on the Feast of Tabernacles, on October 8, 70.[16] The events of 70 A.D. were so significant that by 73 A.D. the history of the Jews became that of the Diaspora, a spreading out of the Jewish nation to Asia, Europe, and Africa. Thereafter, although there would be some remaining elements in the region of their ancestors, they would be a faint shadow of what had once been a vibrant people. As a result of this great scattering, it would become a challenge to identify exactly what event impacting the Jews in various parts of the world coincided with the next four tetrads, which occurred in the years 162-163 AD, 795-796 A.D., 842-843 A.D., and 860-861 A.D.[17] Some efforts to make the connection include a great plague in Europe and a series of Muslim-related events in Europe as well. But by the time the next tetrad arrived in 1493-1494, historical records would allow an easy identification of what great event relating to the Jews the heavens had proclaimed.

The year 1492 is known to many people as the year Christopher Columbus discovered America, establishing that land existed far to the west of the European continent across the great sea. That land, destined to become the United States of America, would also become a safe haven for people from all nations, seeking a better life or escape from persecution. But in that year something else was also happening: the beginning of the monstrous Spanish Inquisition, a violent effort to rid Spain of "infidels."[18] It became a pogrom against the Jews of the most extreme nature, eventually either killing or driving out Jews who did not convert to Catholicism. Columbus would write about it in his journal.

In the same month in which their Majesties [Ferdinand and
Isabella] issued the edict that all Jews should be driven out of
the kingdom and its territories, in the same month they gave
me the order to undertake with sufficient men my expedition
of discovery to the Indies.[19]

This expulsion of the Jews from Spain, so cataclysmic, is noted in
their history as an event almost as important for them, as the discovery of America is in United States history. Those Jews who would not
convert had to depart their homes, forced to sell the accumulation of
generations of family wealth at fire-sale pricing, bringing many into a
state of poverty over the ensuing years. Tens of thousands of the fleeing Jews died in their effort to reach safety. Taking cruel advantage of
desperate people, captains of ships charged frightened Jews exorbitant
fees to become a passenger, only to throw many overboard while out
at sea.[20]

Under the conditions of such a violent purge, rumors become the
norm, with the minds of those participating open to every form of dark
thinking. Claims that fleeing Jews had swallowed diamonds and pieces of
gold, attempting to avoid their confiscation, ran wild. As a result, a new
level of madness began to appear, causing knives to be used on them in an
effort to find the illusionary treasure.[21]

In the years following the great purge, life would be a struggle for
those who escaped. But, ironically, the discovery of America in that same
year would, ultimately, provide them a new safe haven in the future.
And as for Christopher Columbus, credited with discovery of the New
World, there are intriguing new historical documents which suggest he
was secretly a Jew during that terrible time. His last will and testament, as
well as his letters to prominent Jews reporting the progress of his expedi-
tions, even referring to them as his "backers," would be found to support
the contention.

But there is also something else of note concerning this historically significant event for the Jews. Although there had not been a tetrad in more than 632 years, one took place in the years 1493-94, thus, marking the great event.

However, the next tetrad would not occur for another 455 years, taking place in the years 1949 and 1950. But to appreciate the extent of the Jewish event that took place in those years, one must go back to the time of 70 A.D. once again, and the terrible event that plunged the Jews into the Diaspora.

The Jews under the yoke of Rome had been in a state of revolt against their masters, facing 60,000 troops under the Roman general Titus, sent to break the back of their rebellion. Finally, after a five-month siege of the fortified city of Jerusalem, the defensive parameter erected by the Jews around the city broke. And with this break in its defenses, hordes of Roman soldiers began pouring in.[22] Eventually they would reach the holy second Temple. Known to religious Jews as the Holy of Holies, it was more precious to most than their lives. Josephus Flavius, a Jewish historian who lived during the time, recorded what happened after the break occurred.

> ... in hot pursuit right up to the Temple itself. Then one of the soldiers, without awaiting any orders and with no dread of so momentous a deed, but urged on by some supernatural force, snatched a blazing piece of wood and, climbing on another soldier's back, hurled the flaming brand through a low golden window that gave access, on the north side, to the rooms that surrounded the sanctuary. As the flames shot up, the Jews let out a shout of dismay that matched the tragedy; they flocked to the rescue, with no thought of sparing their lives or husbanding their strength; for the sacred structure that they had constantly guarded with such devotion was vanishing before their very eyes.[23]

The result was not only the destruction of the second Temple, but the dispersion of the Jews from their homeland to the four corners of the Earth, just as had been prophesized. Consider this prophecy from the Book of Deuteronomy.

> And the LORD shall scatter thee among all people, from the one end of the earth even unto the other; and there thou shalt serve other gods, which neither thou nor thy fathers have known, even wood and stone. And among these nations shalt thou find no ease, neither shall the sole of thy foot have rest: but the LORD shall give thee there a trembling heart, and failing of eyes, and sorrow of mind: And thy life shall hang in doubt before thee; and thou shalt fear day and night, and shalt have none assurance of thy life:[24]

As history records, this dispersion took place just as was foretold. Along with it their generations would experience the other part of the prophecy, having to "fear day and night, and shalt have none assurance of thy life." Those Jews who went through the Spanish Inquisition understood this well. The scattering of the Jews across the world would last until the year 1948, when their posterity, whom had gathered within the land of their forefathers, fought to establish the nation of Israel again. In spite of the great odds of winning their war for independence against the combined armies of numerous Arab nations, victory came their way in fulfillment of another prophecy. There are numerous prophecies that foretold the reemergence of Israel again as a nation after a time of great dispersion. Perhaps the best known is the one referred to as "The Valley of Dry Bones." Here is a part of it.

> Then he said unto me, Son of man, these bones are the whole house of Israel: behold, they say, Our bones are dried, and our hope is lost: we are cut off for our parts. Therefore prophesy

and say unto them, Thus saith the Lord GOD; Behold, O my people, I will open your graves, and cause you to come up out of your graves, and bring you into the land of Israel. And ye shall know that I am the LORD, when I have opened your graves, O my people, and brought you up out of your graves.[25]

After their declaration of independence in May 1948, and the war that followed, peace came in 1949 along with the fact of their existence back in the land for the first time since the year 70 A.D. The maps of the world had changed, with Israel a nation again for the first time since their brutal scattering by the Romans. And, indeed, the heavens had announced the great event, with the rare tetrad occurring in the years 1949 and 1950.

But another prophecy in the Book of Luke would allude to something else of significance that was about to happen. After their reappearing in the land, the possibility existed that a particular biblical time frame was on the verge of ending, which meant another was about to begin.

And they shall fall by the edge of the sword, and shall be led away captive into all nations: and Jerusalem shall be trodden down of the Gentiles, until the time of the Gentiles be fulfilled.[26]

In 1949, after the dust and fog of war had settled, although the nation of Israel was reborn, the city of Jerusalem remained divided, with the Jews holding only the western sector of the city, the Muslims the eastern side. The "times of the Gentiles" had not yet ended, with the city still being "trodden down" by them. However, with the advances of astronomy and computer technology, suddenly, the ability to project the movement of the heavens into the future was available to the knowing of man. With that knowledge came an understanding of when the next tetrad would arrive. And those watching did not have to wait long. It would unfold only 17 years after the one in 1949-1950, even though that one had taken

455 years to arrive, and the one before it 632 years. But it was a celestial event established in the heavens from the foundation of time, and the speed of its arrival would soon be understood. Its arrival was scheduled to take place in the years 1967 and 1968 and would mark another grand event relating to the Jews.[27]

Since its declaration of independence in 1948 and the war that immediately followed, the nation of Israel experienced very difficult relations with the nations surrounding it. In the 1960s that unpleasant reality would remain. However, as 1967 arrived, the possibility of another war with their neighbors would become a probability. Gamal Abdel Nasser, the leader of Egypt in that day, began taking steps to fulfill multiple promises to Muslims that he would be the one to "drive Israel into the sea." As the month of May arrived, visible steps by Egypt to accomplish that dire goal were seen being taken. Not only was Egypt beginning preparation for war, but Syria as well.[28]

On May 15, 1967, a day marking Israel's 19th anniversary of independence, Egyptian troops began moving throughout the Sinai desert, all along their border with Israel. Three days later, on the other side of the small Jewish state, Syrian troops began doing the same, massing and preparing for battle along the strategic Golan Heights. On May 16 Egypt ordered all U.N. peace keeping forces out of the Sinai, warning them that it would soon not be safe to be there. Egyptian government-controlled radio would proudly proclaim their departure, offering this perspective to their listeners.

As of today, there no longer exists an international emergency force to protect Israel. We shall exercise patience no more. We shall not complain any more to the U.N. about Israel. The sole method we shall apply against Israel is total war, which will result in the extermination of Zionist existence.[29]

In Syria its Defense Minister, Hafez Assad, would echo those belligerent words.

Our forces are now entirely ready, not only to repulse the aggression, but to initiate the act of liberation itself, and to explode the Zionist presence in the Arab homeland. The Syrian army, with its finger on the trigger, is united .... I as a military man, believe that the time has come to enter into a battle of annihilation.[30]

With such words came the realistic possibility that Israel was about to be attacked again. So on June 5, 1967, instead of waiting to be attacked, Israel decided to hit first. In an act of military brilliance, every Israeli fighter aircraft that the country possessed, save for only 12 left to defend the skies of Israel, attacked their Egyptian counterparts as their pilots ate breakfast. In order to avoid detection by Egyptian radar, the Israeli attack force flew across the Mediterranean Sea at the height of waves and when they reached Egyptian waters, turned inland, going directly to all Egyptian Air Force bases. What they found there was stunning. Lined up one after another in neat and orderly columns on each runway was the entire Egyptian Air Force. With their planes wing to wing, it was a turkey-shoot quickly resulting in the destruction of more than 300 military fighter aircraft.[31] After the carnage was over, the Egyptian Air Force was no longer a military factor. Only two hours after that great accomplishment, the Israeli Air Force went after the Jordanian and Syrian air forces, with much the same result.

With their air power destroyed within just a matter of hours, the Muslim armies on the ground that were prepared to attack Israel had little chance, and within four days they were destroyed by Israeli armored columns. Israel had, once again, won the right to exist. But within the battle something viewed by many Israelis as more important than the smashing victory itself had taken place. Since it was Jordan that controlled East Jerusalem and had made the fateful decision to join Egypt and Syria in their war against Israel, Jewish troops captured East Jerusalem, uniting the city for the first time in almost 2,000 years.[32] And with the uniting of the City of Jerusalem, no longer was it "trodden down" by the Gentiles, indicating the completion of the "time of the Gentiles be fulfilled."

Those who had considered what the heavenly tetrad in 1967-1968 would signify no longer had to wonder. It marked one of the most significant events in Jewish history; the restoration of Jerusalem to the new state of Israel. And although on average a tetrad had occurred only once every 323 years between the death of Jesus and the reestablishment of the nation of Israel, there had been only a 17-year period between this one and the last. And within that small time frame came the perfect heavenly alert to those understanding the sign.

By using those same computer models to look into the future, it would not be long, once again, before the next astronomical/religiously rare event of a tetrad would take place. This one would arrive in the years 2014 and 2015 and, once again, leave those aware of its approach to wonder what stark prophetic event it too would mark. What the previous tetrads showed was that in each case where records were available, it marked something significant for the Jews, either very positive or very negative.

There is much written in the ancient Scriptures that relates to signs in the heavens. In the Book of Luke, after the passage relating to the changing of the times from that of the Gentiles, to that of Israel, this passage immediately follows it:

> And there shall be signs in the sun, and in the moon, and in the stars; and upon the earth distress of nations, with perplexity; the sea and the waves roaring;[33]

The coming tetrad in the years 2014 and 2015 will be the first since "the time of the Gentiles [were] fulfilled" in 1967, and eerily fulfilling the sequence of events the reader is told to look for. In another Scripture referring to events leading up to the "day of the Lord," this from the Book of Joel:

And I will shew wonders in the heavens and in the earth, blood, and fire, and pillars of smoke. The sun shall be turned into darkness, and the moon into blood, before the great and terrible day of the LORD come.[34]

So not only are we alerted to look for the blood moons, "and the moon into blood," and the eclipse of the Sun causing it to be "turned into darkness," but other "wonders in the heavens." It would appear that the point of these Scriptures is to alert the reader to look for a sequence of celestial events that will occur after the "time of the Gentiles be fulfilled." If that is so, then there should be other interesting celestial events leading up to the coming tetrad.

Wonders in the Heavens

Across the skies of Russia, near the city of Chelyabinsk on February 18, 2013, a heavenly event took place that had not been seen on planet Earth since the huge meteor that crashed near the forest at "Tungska," Russia in the year 1908. Its arrival over Chelyabinsk would set the Internet and TV ablaze with images of a fireball streaking through the sky, the likes of which no one alive could remember ever having seen. The object in question, described as a small asteroid approximately 55 to 65 feet in size, roared through the atmosphere at a high rate of speed and at a shallow angle, producing an enormous amount of energy in its wake. Its explosion 18 miles in the atmosphere disturbed the pressure in the area to an extent that it caused the shattering of windows within a large radius, sending glass hurling at those in its way. The result was more than 1,300 individuals needing hospital care for injuries. And it is no wonder things went flying. It is estimated that the energy radiated from the space rock entering the atmosphere was similar to what would be released from a 440-kiloton nuclear weapon being detonated.[35] Although the Russian asteroid made headlines across the globe because of its exceedingly rare nature, astronomers were ready for other heavenly visitors scheduled to arrive in the year 2013.

The online magazine Universe Today would sum it up in its headline: "The Year of the Comets: Three Reasons Why 2013 Could be the Best Ever." The reason for that optimism centers on three comets that will be visible to the naked eye, making the year a comet anomaly, with the last comet set to arrive later in the year and possibly one of historic brilliance. One, named 4L PANSTARS, brought along its fan-shaped dust tail the size of two full moons' diameter long, dazzling those who knew where to look for it. Another, named F6 Lemmon, although barely visible to the naked eye, was another show for those knowing where to look. But it is the final comet of the year that is the real show-stopper.[36]

The headline of an online article by FOX News would say it all: "2013 comet may be brightest ever seen." And indeed, the arrival of comet ISON, expected to be visible in October, November, and December, will not only allow easy naked-eye viewing in the night sky, but during the day as well. In fact, it is expected that in the middle of the day, along with the sun in the sky, this heavenly spectacle with its long tail will be competing for attention.[37] And it is interesting that such a year of comets, which are certainly heavenly wonders, would begin in the year before the coming tetrad is set to start unfolding.

CHAPTER SIX

Wars and Rumors of Wars

A s the Israeli spy moved about within the computer systems of the Iranian nuclear complex, what he was about to do would represent a new form of warfare. It would also add another weapon to the vast array already existing in mankind's arsenal dedicated against one another. And in this case the actual attack was one where the intended target would not even know what had happened until sometime much later ... too late for them, hopefully.[1] The attack would not come from a bomb or bullets, which would be far too obvious. It would come from an object never before associated with warfare: a simple computer stick, or flash drive.

It wasn't just any computer stick the spy was carrying, but one that possessed code so complicated it took the Herculean efforts of a government and the best programmers to construct. It was a new form of warfare, one that combatants of days past would not have recognized. As the small device was placed within the proper computer portal, its disruptive series of numbers and code began pouring into the Iranian computer systems at a furious pace.[2,3] They were systems dedicated to building a nuclear bomb, which then could be dedicated to the destruction of the hated Jews and their nation Israel. But like poison slowly entering the blood stream of its victim, the Mullahs in Tehran would not even know it was there until outward signs began appearing several years later. Hopefully, by then it would be too late and their coveted nuclear program would be severely damaged.

The attack, which apparently took place in 2007, would slow down the Iranian drive for nuclear weapons, but not stop it. As a program dedicated to advancing Iran into the nuclear club, it is the nation of Israel that has been the most concerned, and for good reason. Statements coming out of the repressive regime in Tehran describing Israel as a "cancerous tumor" that must "vanish from the pages of time" have made it clear why Iran needs nuclear weapons.[4] And the litany of angry words against Israel coming from the Islamist regime in Iran would highlight a sense of threat that would begin a unique time of rumors that war between the two would occur at any time.

Mahmoud Ahmadinejad, president of Iran until June 2013, has been the source of lengthy threats against Israel, with words that are seldom heard in disputes between nations. His speeches would include calls to "eliminate the Zionist regime." He would question that the Holocaust had ever happened. He would eagerly support a protest called "A world without Zionism," inferring the end of Israel as a nation. He would claim that the Jews have no history in Palestine, or, as he would put it, "have no roots in Palestine," and urge European nations to parcel tracts of land within their own countries for the Jews to move into as they depart Palestine.[5] And condemnations of such remarks came from an array of European Foreign Ministers, demanding they have "no place in civilized political debate." But Ahmadinejad did not curtail his threats. On Israel's 60th birthday, he would offer these words to his regional neighbor.

Those who think they can revive the stinking corpse of the usurping and fake Israeli regime by throwing a birthday party are seriously mistaken. Today the reason for the Zionist regime's existence is questioned, and this regime is on its way to annihilation."[6]

But to make certain no one missed the point he was making, the Iranian leader would add that Israel "has reached the end like a dead rat after being slapped by the Lebanese." Not long after those words were spoken, he said, "The Zionist regime is dying," and "The criminals imagine that by holding celebrations they can save the Zionist regime from death." Ahmadinejad also stated that "They should know that regional nations hate this fake and criminal regime and if the smallest and briefest chance is given to regional nations they will destroy (it)." And to cap it all off, before the United Nations he would declare that "today the Zionist regime is on a definite slope to collapse."[7] And the litany of hate would go on and on.

As sponsor of the Qods Day, a gathering dedicated to the removal of Israel from Jerusalem, in July 2012, Ahmdainejad stated that "any freedom lover and justice seeker in the world must do its best for the annihilation of the Zionist regime in order to pave the path for the establishment of justice and freedom in the world," and that the ultimate objective of world forces must be the annihilation of the "Zionist regime." The next month he pointed out to those with ears to hear that "the very existence of the Zionist regime is an insult to humanity."[8] And as these terrible threats have been spoken against Israel, the Iranian nuclear program continued to advance.

It would take only one nuclear bomb detonated within the tiny Jewish nation to accomplish Ahmadinejad's stated goals. But of course, they are the goals of the leadership of Iran, not just that single man. And in spite of Iran electing a new president, Hassan Rohani, the real power and direction of the nation still rests in the hands of its radical Supreme Leader, Ayatollah Ali Kahmenei. As a result, the rumor of war between the two regional powers, Israel and Iran, has been present since the early 2000s. In fact, it is difficult to find another instance in the twentieth century where so strong a rumor of war persisted for so many years. And the litany of rumors would be impressive.

In the year 2003, a Scottish newspaper indicated Israel:

is prepared to take unilateral military action against Iran if necessary if the international community fails to stop any development of nuclear weapons at the country's atomic energy facilities.[6]

As a result, many analysts began considering that an Israeli attack could happen any time in that year, knowing how Israel in years past had reached out great distances against other foes also attempting to develop a nuclear weapons program. Such an attack had taken place against Iraq and its Osirak nuclear facility in 1981. And years later it would be repeated against the Syrian effort at al-Kibar in 2007.[7,8] Since in both cases Israel had struck without warning, reasonable people believed the small Jewish state would not hesitate to do so again against Iran. In both of those previous attacks there had been no rumors preceding the assault: only the attacks themselves would alert the world that combat had taken place between Israel and an Arab foe.

But with Iran this would not be the case. Although in the case of Iraq and Syria, neither made sport of threatening the existence of Israel, and yet was attacked to prevent them from grasping nuclear weapons capability: Iran was a different matter. With its leadership embracing the strange Twelvers sect of Islam, which includes the necessity of bringing about great death and destruction to fulfill their religious duty, the need for nuclear weapons was clear.[10] Therefore, many Middle East watchers believed it was inevitable that Israel would attack the Iranian nuclear facilities, resulting in a devastating regional war. This reasoning was especially viewed as valid since the Persian regime had specifically singled out Israel for mass destruction in line with its end time belief system. But no attack took place in that year. However, various newspapers across the globe continued to pick up on rumors of an inevitable war between the two nations.

In 2005 it would be the turn of a British paper indicating that then Israeli Prime Minister, Ariel Sharon, had ordered the military to draft plans for strikes against Iranian uranium enrichment locations spread out across the large country. In 2006 it was indicated that Iran was within 2-4 years of being able to build a nuclear weapon. As a result, it was reported that the Israeli Special Forces command was placed in the highest stage of readiness with their target the Iranian nuclear facilities. In that same year, Symore Hersh, reporting for CNN, uncovered that the Bush Administration had been carrying out secret reconnaissance missions within Iran to learn more about their nuclear program, with the intent of being ready to attack them. Mr. Hersh indicated that U.S. officials were involved in "extensive planning" for a possible attack, "much more than we know." Then this:

> The goal is to identify three dozen, and perhaps more, such targets that could be destroyed by precision strikes and short-term commando raids.[10]

The U.S. administration would deny it. Then, later that year, responding to the continuous flow of Iranian threats to bring another Holocaust down upon the Jews, Israeli Vice Premier, Shimon Perez, pointed out to Iranian leaders that "when it comes to destruction, Iran too can be destroyed." He added that "Israel would defend itself under any condition."[11] All of this, and much more, would be heard by those following the possibility of war between Iran and Israel. But as 2005 and 2006 came and then departed, all of it would remain nothing more than rumors of an attack that would result in war.

THE COMING MIDEAST WAR AND PEACE TREATY

In 2007 Iranian leaders talked about their response to any potential Israeli or American attack against them, boasting of their ability to cause great damage to the United States Persian Gulf fleet, as well as their ability to close the vitally important Strait of Hormuz, where over 20% of the world's oil passes each day. Ali Shirazi, an aide to Iran's supreme leader, put a voice to the Iranian side of things.

> The first US shot against Iran would set the United States' vital interests in the world on fire ... Tel Aviv and the US fleet in the Persian Gulf would be the targets that would be set on fire in Iran's crushing response.[12]

Yet, for all of the rumors, no shots were fired.

In 2009 the British Guardian newspaper reported that United Nations nuclear watchdog agency was asking Iran why it was experimenting with advanced warhead design, if, as it had been claiming, its goal was for only the peaceful use of nuclear power. It would also come out in that year from documents published by the International Atomic Energy Agency that Iranian scientists had tested components of a "two-point implosion" device. Such a device is only usable in the detonation process of a nuclear weapon. And within this environment of continuous war talk without it happening, Israeli Deputy Foreign Minister Danny Ayalon would stress that no one should take that to mean Israel would not do what it needed to when the time came.[13] And with that, and other statements, the rumor of an impending Middle Eastern war between Israel and Iran continued.

In 2010, 2011, 2012, and 2013, claims of preparations for war against Iran by Israel included their receiving special bunker-busting bombs necessary to penetrate into deep underground bunkers, the kind that Iran had constructed to protect their growing nuclear enrichment facilities.[14] Also, flotillas of naval warships from an array of allied nations would be sent to the Persian Gulf, appearing at the ready to keep the strategic Persian Gulf open for shipping should Iran attempt to close it as punishment for an Israeli attack.[15] In spite of all this, nothing would happen, even as the prospect of a major, even regional war in the Middle East became a rumor mill of the first order. In spite of there being no major war, the signs of conflict between the two nations continued to be seen.

In addition to a virus being pumped into the Iranian nuclear computer system, successfully damaging mechanical devices associated with it, other unfriendly actions were taking place against them. Between 2007 and 2011, four Iranian scientists working on the nuclear program were assassinated by the use of bombs, gunshots, or poison.[16] A fifth would barely survive a car bombing. After one success, the Times of London reported from an unnamed Israeli source that the assassination was done as a prelude to an all-out attack.[17] And this, of course, cranked up the rumor mill again. However, the attack never came. The article also actually detailed the steps taken to kill one scientist, in what appeared to be a purposeful effort to enrage the Iranians. It worked, but there was still no war, only the continuous rumor that it was near.

In 2013 the new Secretary of Defense for the United States publicly assured Israel that the Iranian nuclear threat was seen "exactly the same" by both countries. Then he stressed that Israel has the right to defend itself, a code term for attack Iran, causing the rumors of an impending war to grow ever louder.[18] Adding fuel to that fire was an enormous sale of U.S. arms to Israel, including long-range refueling planes necessary for distant attacks against such long-range targets as Iran. Such planes appeared to fill a critical Israeli weakness in going great distances to attack. Those questioning the timing of the sale of arms to the Jewish state received the response from the Defense Secretary that the question of whether or not to attack was an Israeli "calculation." He would add, "Israel is a sovereign nation; every sovereign nation has a right to defend itself."[19] And the rumors of war whipped up again.

THE COMING MIDEAST WAR AND PEACE TREATY

Articles in major publications with such titles as, "Will this be the year that Israel goes to war with Iran,"[20] and "Is war between Israel and Iran inevitable,"[21] marked headlines in 2013. And for at least ten years, since 2003, year-by-year, tremendous media would be dedicated to speculation on war breaking out at any moment between Israel and Iran. Yet, at no time since Israel's 1949 founding has there been such rumors of war for anywhere near this length of time. Not only have bellicose words been exchanged for a length of time creating this rumor mill of war, but also, the devastating potential such a war would have added to the stress of it all.

The potential cost of a war between Israel and Iran, not only in economic terms but military as well, are truly staggering. War games played out at the Pentagon included the scenario of over 10,000 rockets fired into Israel from Lebanon in the north, compliments of Hezbollah, the terrorist organization that took over there and is heavily supported by Iran. An Israeli general would indicate that 5,000 warheads are capable of actually hitting Tel Aviv.[22] In the south of Israel the terrorist organization, Hamas, would be expected to launch rockets into Israel as well, but not nearly as many. Iran would unleash its long-range rockets packed with high explosives also, aimed not only at Israel, but Gulf region states friendly to the United States. In particular, the oil fields in the region and refining facilities would be targeted. Proxy sleeper cells in Western nations would, in all likelihood, be awakened to strike their rehearsed blows against the Great Satan. And only the order from Tehran would reveal how many had slipped into the nation through its porous southern U.S. border.

In the Persian Gulf, home to over 20% of the world's oil flow, the strategic Strait of Hormuz, its choke point, would likely be immediately closed by an Iranian multi-layered approach. Such actions would probably involve the sinking of large ships in the narrow channel, the release of massive floating mines, and speed boats dedicated to suicide runs against U.S. warships attempting to clear the path. Such speed boats could cost the U.S. fleet dearly by acting in large groups attacking all at once in a swarm, according to war games played out at the Pentagon.[23] In the Middle East region U.S. forces stationed there would probably come under assault, causing the U.S. to become involved even as Israel struck the blow. As the U.S. general in charge of American's Middle East presence stated, such a war would have dire consequences for the United States.[24]

But it is not just the rumors of a great war between the Middle Eastern regional powers of Israel and Iran that has been playing for over a decade. In the case of Israel, it is the fact of war that has been connected to their existence since the nation's founding in 1948. Consider the amazing litany of war after war since their reemergence as a state.[25]

After the declaration of independence that year by the Jews living in the region, a life and death struggle began, which eventually led to the founding of Israel. Arrayed against the Jews were the Arab armies of Egypt, Syria, Jordan, Lebanon, and Iraq. This war is, typically, referred to as the **War for Independence.**

Then in the 1950s and 1960s Israel found itself still in a constant state of conflict with Arab guerillas infiltrating across the border through Syria, Egypt, and Jordan. The goal of these guerillas, or fedayeen, was to kill civilians and soldiers as the opportunity presented itself. Imagine having roving bands of gunmen seeking any man, woman, or child as their target in your neighborhood. Those living in Israel at the time did not have to imagine it, they lived it. As a result, Israel began a series of "reprisal operations" dedicated to punishing those gathered on the other side of the border who were preparing to strike. This war is referred to as the **reprisal operations.**

In October of 1956, Israel was involved in a war with both France and Britain directed at maintaining free passage through the Suez Canal. At the end of it all the Jews had effectively secured their southern border. This war is referred to as the **Suez Crisis.**

71

THE COMING MIDEAST WAR AND PEACE TREATY

In June of 1967, Israel struck the coiled armies of Egypt, Syria, and Jordan, assisted by troops from Saudi Arabia, Kuwait, and Algeria. This first strike against those armies was out of the fear that if they struck Israel first the Jews would be defeated. In the aftermath of that war Israel gained control over a considerable amount of land from the nations on her borders. This war is referred to as the **Six-Day War.**

Between 1967 and 1970, after the entire Sinai desert was lost to Israel, Egypt with the assistance of Syria, Jordan, the USSR, and the Palestinian Liberation Organization, fought a limited war against the Israeli troops positioned in the Sinai to retain control over it. Eventually, a cease-fire ended hostilities, with the frontiers remaining in the same place as when the war began. This war is referred to as the **War of Attrition.**

On October 6, 1973, Egypt and Syria struck Israel in a surprise attack as a way of recapturing the lands lost in their 1967 debacle. Although initially caught off-guard, Israel rebounded with the help of a massive American airlift of tanks and other supplies. After the war was over, there were no significant territorial changes. This war is referred to as the **Yom Kippur War.**

After the Palestinian Liberation Organization moved its military wing into South Lebanon from Jordan, strikes into Israel began taking place on a regular basis. In response, Israeli retaliation became the norm from 1971 until 1982. This conflict is referred to as the **Palestinian Insurgency in South Lebanon.**

After over ten years of fighting the Palestinian insurgency in South Lebanon, Israel decided to launch an invasion there to rid the region of hostile forces once and for all. After it was over Israel had secured a security buffer zone. This war is referred to as the **1982 Lebanon War.**

The war in South Lebanon did not stop with the Israeli establishment of the buffer zone. It continued as a low-intensity war and is, generally speaking, referred to as the **South Lebanon Conflict.**

With a large Arab Palestinian population in the area typically referred to as the West Bank, attacks against Israeli troops stationed there turned into a mass uprising referred to as the **First Intifada.** This took place between 1987 and 1993. Not many years later the **Second Intifada** was launched, taking place between 2000 and 2005.

In 2006, with Lebanon still a festering source of attacks, Israeli Defense Forces entered south Lebanon for the second time to rid the area of forces fighting for the terrorist group called Hezbollah. After it ended it was referred to as the **Second Lebanon War.**

With Hamas in charge of the strip of land between Southern Israel and the Sinai desert called Gaza, the Muslim Brotherhood offshoot would continuously attack Israel with rockets. The attacks came in spite of the fact that Israel had ceded control of Gaza to the Palestinians in August 2005 in an act many had hoped would bring peace there. After realizing it had the opposite effect, Israeli forces launched en masse into the area in December 2008. This war is referred to as the **Gaza War.** They would find the need to do it again in November 2012 under **Operation Pillar of Defense.**

If the above litany makes it appear that Israel has been in a state of war since its founding in 1948, it should, because it has. It includes The War for Independence, Reprisal Operations, Suez Crisis, Six-Day War, War of Attrition, Yom Kippur War, and Palestinian Insurgency in Southern Lebanon, 1982 Lebanon War, South Lebanon Conflict, First Intifada, Second Intifada, 2006 Lebanon War, Gaza War, and Operation Pillar of Defense.[26] Considering that there are only 65 years between 1948 when the Jews declared their independence and the year 2013, yet 14 wars have been fought, this equals Israel going to war on average about once every four-and-a-half years! In fact, adding to those wars are the countless one-day attacks launched by Israel against various threats.

When a nation goes to war, its population will talk of little else but that conflict for a period of time. As a result, it is those living within

73

the nation at war that hear the most about "war." Therefore, since being founded in 1948, those living in Israel have heard the constant drumbeat of war. However, since the early 2000s there has been a new element added to the mix. Since that time rumors of a major regional war pitting Israel against Iran, and a host of their allies such as Hezbollah in Lebanon and Hamas in Gaza, has now been heard as well. And it has been playing like a broken record while all the time defying the best analysis of when it will transform from a rumor into an actual war. In the twentieth century there appears nothing quite like it. So it is within Israel since their founding where the population has heard of war on a constant basis, with the "rumors of wars" added as well. And the extent of which Israel has experienced this is unmatched by any other nation on Earth.

* * * * *

There are verses of Scripture located in the Book of Matthew, chapter 24, where Jesus provides a description of certain signs that will appear prior to the end of the age. And it is His words so carefully placed near the beginning of this text that draws our attention.

> [4] And Jesus answered and said unto them, Take heed that no man deceive you. [5] For many shall come in my name, saying, I am Christ; and shall deceive many.

> [6] And ye shall hear of wars and rumors of wars: see that ye be not troubled: for all these things must come to pass, but the end is not yet.

> [7] For nation shall rise against nation, and kingdom against kingdom: and there shall be famines, and pestilences, and earthquakes, in diverse places.

> [8] All these are the beginning of sorrows.[27]

Consider Verses 4-5

> [4] And Jesus answered and said unto them, Take heed that no man deceive you. [5] For many shall come in my name, saying, I am Christ; and shall deceive many.

Some see this Scripture as being fulfilled by those few and strange characters, here and there, that claim to be Christ today. And there are, indeed, a few such individuals making this claim. There have also been such individuals, here and there, over the course of the last several centuries that have made these claims as well. And, perhaps, they are exactly what the Scripture is telling us to look for. However, if that is the case then it would appear a little difficult to use it as a signpost of the times because the phenomenon has been going on for a while. And yet there are not so many of these characters present today as to be noteworthy, or to justify the term "many" to be applied to them as a group. If such characters are what we are to specifically look for, then to be able to distinguish it as a sign warned of would require a dramatic increase in these Christ claims in order to clearly identify that the warning is suddenly unfolding. Although this may be what we are to look for, here is another way to consider the biblical warning being provided in those verses.

If a man is sent out among the people to read a proclamation from the king, and instead of reading the words given him, replaces them with his own words, has not that man placed himself in the role of the king deceiving many? And so it is with those vested with the responsibility of speaking the words of God today. Are not many in that role blatantly replacing God's words with their own? Are there not some who claim to represent Christ saying a man can marry another man, and that God approves? Are they not placing themselves as Christ in that moment, and do they not deceive many? "They come in [His] name," and by changing His words are effectively saying "I am Christ," and they "deceive many."

75

It's just some food for thought that there are a lot more "Christ's" running around than we may realize.

Consider Verse 6

> [6] And ye shall hear of wars and rumors of wars: see that ye be not troubled: for all these things must come to pass, but the end is not yet.

Many who have studied this Scripture believe it refers to a time where <u>across the Earth</u> the scene will be notable for how many "wars and rumors of wars" are occurring. And it is that sign associated with this Scripture which appears to be the key in identifying the time is at hand. But for those today who are looking for this sign being fulfilled by nations <u>across the Earth</u>, indicating that the end of the age is approaching, that perspective has a real problem. The problem would be heralded in a 2011 headline from *The New York Times* that would say it all: "War Really Is Going Out of Style."[28] And based on statistics, this would appear to be the case. When looking at wars <u>across the Earth,</u> they peaked long ago and have been declining ever since. Actually, the graph charting it looks like a stock market that crashed, with a strong case to be made that war in the twentieth century began declining since the 1950s. By looking at the average number of conflicts per year between nation states as well as civil wars, on a decade-by-decade basis after World War II, it is the decade of the 1950s which stands out as a peak from which they have declined ever since. In addition to the number of conflicts being in sharp decline, the intensity of those occurring has also dropped dramatically, peaking in the 1950s. This is an <u>across the Earth</u> average.

Here is a graph of the international conflicts since the decade of the 1950s. As is obvious from that decade forward, the headline in the Times appears to be on to something.

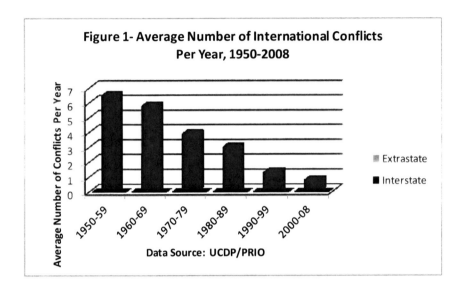

Figure 1- Average Number of International Conflicts Per Year, 1950-2008

Average Number of Conflicts Per Year

Extrastate
Interstate

1950-59 1960-69 1970-79 1980-89 1990-99 2000-08

Data Source: UCDP/PRIO

It is difficult to argue with the numbers, and the decline is so dramatic as to have caused scholars to debate the reasons for the sharp and steady drop. It is easy to observe that the European nations, which used to go to war against one another at the least provocation, have not had a war since 1945. And the decline is not just in such major conflicts between nation states, but civil wars and small localized conflicts. Civil wars have become fewer, smaller, and fought on a more localized level. Political scientist John Mueller, in his paper titled, "The Demise of War and of Speculation About The Causes Thereof," would add his thoughts to the mix, noting how many civil wars have evolved into something that tends to resemble competing gangs, thugs, and organized crime units usually referred to as "armed militias."[29] In many cases such "civil wars" are fought over control of illegal drugs or by religious fanatics seeking tribute. Also notable is how not only has the number of wars declined sharply, but the overall number of deaths related to battle has done so as well, as indicated by the following chart.

THE COMING MIDEAST WAR AND PEACE TREATY

Beginning in the 1950s, it is apparent, here too, that deaths associated with war have plunged to levels difficult to imagine could ever happen.

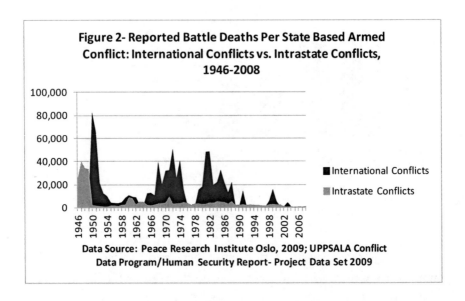

Figure 2- Reported Battle Deaths Per State Based Armed Conflict: International Conflicts vs. Intrastate Conflicts, 1946-2008

Data Source: Peace Research Institute Oslo, 2009; UPPSALA Conflict Data Program/Human Security Report- Project Data Set 2009

This graph of reported battle deaths confirms the previous graph that the decline began in the decade of the 1950s. Since both are considering the same phenomenon but from different perspectives, they appear to be telling the same story.

Since the year 1600 B.C., there have been more than 14,000 wars, and they have taken the lives of countless people <u>across the Earth</u>. And although the two world wars in the twentieth century were the most deadly in history, it is that fact which makes them so notable. Overall in recent decades the annual rate of battle deaths worldwide, based on every 100,000 of world population has plunged. During World War II it stood at about 300, during the Korean War it dropped to about 30, and then into the low teens during Vietnam. In the 1970s and 1980s, it dropped into the single digits. And then, as the world entered the twenty-first century, it plunged all the way down to less than one battle death for every 100,000 in population.[30] So by any measure, if the Scripture alerting the reader to look for "wars and rumors of wars" pertains to nations <u>across the Earth</u>, then it simply is not being fulfilled today.

Considering these data, it is obvious that from a historical perspective, on an <u>across the Earth</u> basis, since the middle of the twentieth century, war has almost been eliminated. In fact, the nations <u>across the Earth</u> appear to be in an almost eerie state of peace with one another. Yes, there are still conflicts in various places, and they make it to the TV screen often giving the false appearance that much conflict is taking place. But from a historical perspective, that impression is completely false.

However, by considering verses 6, 7, and 8 together, there is a perspective relating to the meaning of these verses that appears to be getting perfectly fulfilled today. In fact, it could only become perfectly fulfilled at such a time as this.

Matthew 24:6-8

[6] And ye shall hear of <u>wars and rumors of wars</u>: see that ye be not troubled: for all these things must come to pass, but the end is not yet. (Emphasis added)

[7] For <u>nation shall rise against nation</u>, and kingdom against kingdom: and there shall be famines, and pestilences, and earthquakes, in diverse places. (Emphasis added)

[8] All these are the beginning of sorrows.

Again, for those who embrace the perspective that <u>"wars and rumors of wars"</u> pertain to nations <u>across the Earth</u>, there is a redundancy here they must deal with. After telling the reader to look for "wars and rumors of wars" in verse 6, in the next verse we are told that the next thing to look for is, "nation shall rise against nation," which certainly does represent war across the Earth. So if the wars mentioned in verse 6 also represent those among nations across the Earth, then who is left to fulfill verse 7. In other words, if the nations across the Earth are already at war in verse 6, why mention "nation shall rise against nation" in verse 7. And who is left to rise at that point? The more logical perspective here is that the "wars and rumors of wars" pertain to the condition of restored Israel, not the nations across the Earth. The nations across the Earth are then handled in the next verse, "nation shall rise against nation," where, obviously, a great war breaks out among them. It is only Israel today that has been embroiled in a constant state of "wars" since being founded with, amazingly, a new war breaking out on average every 4.6 years since 1948. And as for "rumors of wars" (Iran, Lebanon, and Gaza), it is Israel that has experienced this phenomenon more than any other nation in the twentieth century, the likes of which has been as persistent as it has been imminent for over a decade.

For about a decade the world has been waiting for an Israeli-Iranian war to break out at any moment. Wow, what a rumor of war. Now ponder the following question. Can you remember any time in your life where the rumor of an imminent war between two nations has persisted for as long as ten years? And if you are thinking of the Cold War, don't. The only time the rumor of war came out in that standoff was during short-lived challenges between the Soviet Union and the United States centered on such events as the Berlin Airlift and the Cuban Missile Crisis, with both only lasting a short time.

Also, remember, when Jesus is speaking these words it is to a group of Jews, so when He tells them they would hear of "wars and rumors of wars" they had to think He was talking about Israel. Since He was speaking directly to a group of Jews, how could those present not take that warning as relating to them as a people? He is telling them that when there are "wars and rumors of wars" to be alert. Would He really tell them such a thing if it related to some other people? And if it did relate to another people would He not have specified what other peoples to watch for this unfolding sign? The Jews present during this discourse must have inherently understood that He was talking about a condition of Israel, at some point in the future, especially since in His next sentence He then singles out the nations as where the next event in the sequence will unfold.

Another perspective here is that the world is divided into two groups: one being Israel and the other the nations of the world. Notice also that in verse 6, after alerting the reader to look for "wars and rumors of wars," it is stated that "the end is not yet." In other words, it demarcates a time frame that has not yet begun, but is obviously close. This is distinguished from the next verse, 7, wherein there is a litany of events described in which verse 8 indicates the beginning of the end, or, "sorrows." So one appears to demarcate the time just before the beginning of the end, and the other demarcates the actual beginning phase of it. They appear to be in chronological order here. In other words, the beginning of this prophetic time frame in verse 7 is the start of the biblically warned-of season referred to as the birth pains. Also, the news that "nation shall rise against nation" must be a very notable event because it is followed by the terrible plagues of "famines, and pestilences." It will have to be a truly terrible war that will come upon the world to achieve such notable afflictions, as man has suffered "famines and pestilences" as the norm since his beginning. And since such notable "famines and pestilences" have clearly not taken place yet, it is another reason to view the events described in verse 7 as different from those in verse 6.

There is yet another reason to view the events in verse 7 as not having begun yet, and that is the lack of notable earthquake activity. Although news of earthquakes takes place from time to time, and can give the appearance that they are many, the facts do not confirm that observation. Consider the following chart dating back to the year 1900 and going all the way to the year 1989. It is a year-by-year count of 7.0 or higher quakes. As the data confirm, there is no notable increase that has taken place in that time frame.

Number Of Earthquakes Per Year Magnitude 7.0 Or Greater
1900–1989

1900	13	1930	13	1960	22
1901	14	1931	26	1961	18
1902	8	1932	13	1962	15
1903	10	1933	14	1963	20
1904	16	1934	22	1964	15
1905	26	1935	24	1965	22
1906	32	1936	21	1966	19
1907	27	1937	22	1967	16
1908	18	1938	26	1968	30
1909	32	1939	21	1969	27
1910	36	1940	23	1970	29
1911	24	1941	24	1971	23
1912	22	1942	27	1972	20
1913	23	1943	41	1973	16
1914	22	1944	31	1974	21
1915	18	1945	27	1975	21
1916	25	1946	35	1976	25
1917	21	1947	26	1977	16
1918	21	1948	28	1978	18
1919	14	1949	36	1979	15
1920	8	1950	39	1980	18
1921	11	1951	21	1981	14
1922	14	1952	17	1982	10

1923	23	1953	22	1983	15
1924	18	1954	17	1984	8
1925	17	1955	19	1985	15
1926	19	1956	15	1986	6
1927	20	1957	34	1987	11
1928	22	1958	10	1988	8
1929	19	1959	15	1989	7

Statistics were compiled from the Earthquake Data Base System of the U.S. Geological Survey, National Earthquake Information Center, Golden CO

A perusal of the chart clearly indicates that the number of earthquakes has not increased as the end is approached. Now consider the following graph which tracks earthquakes 5.0 or higher, with dots marking the years they happened. As it too demonstrates, there is no increase that has taken place between the years 1990 and 2012.

Earthquakes Located by the NEIC

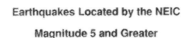

Magnitude 5 and Greater

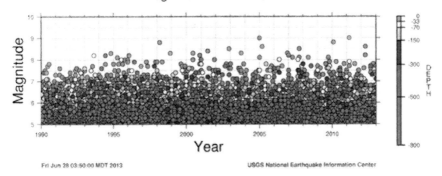

So as it relates to verse 7 in Matthew 24, not only has "nation shall rise against nation" NOT taken place, neither have the earthquakes warned of. Therefore, since that verse marks the "beginning of sorrows," that critical time frame of **birth pains** has not yet begun. However, the moment just before the onset of those **birth pains** as indicated in verse 6, "wars and rumors of wars," is currently being perfectly fulfilled by Israel.

Here is something else to consider. If, indeed, it is Israel that the warning "wars and rumors of wars" is relating to, then the end of those "rumors" of war should mark the completion of the biblical time frame "the end is not yet." Realistically those "rumors" can only end one of two ways. If Israel and Iran make peace, then the "rumors" of war will end. However, for those familiar with the issues between the two nations, a move toward peace appears impossible. The other way for it to end is war. When a rumor of war turns into war, the rumor ends as the war begins. That would appear to be the much more likely ending to the "rumors" and marking an ending of a significant biblical time frame described as "the end is not yet." The next war where, "nation shall rise against nation" will happen sometime after the Israel-Iran war.

With there being so few nations warring against other nations at present, the world is in a state of relative peace. From a historical perspective this perfectly places them in the position to rise up against one another when the biblically warned-of verse 7 arrives declaring that "nation shall rise against nation." Remember, a nation cannot rise up that has already risen. So if verse 6 relates to the condition of Israel, then the nations of the world are perfectly placed to rise up in verse 7. Not only that, but since the state of peace among nations is possibly greater than at any time in man's history, then the stage is set for the greatest rise against one another there has ever been.

Because since its founding Israel has experienced constant wars, and now the litany of rumors of wars relating to Iran and her allies on Israel's borders, where does that place mankind in the scheme of things? To answer that question it places the world in the "wars and rumors of wars" "but the end is not yet" phase. That means the next prophetic event is for the "rumors" to end, which appears to mean an actual war between Israel and Iran.

CHAPTER SEVEN

The Coming Middle East Crisis

President Obama's Middle Eastern policies have often taken on a confusing appearance during his first term in office, either wittingly, or unwittingly, setting the stage for tremendous pressure to become focused on Israel. Part of this is because Israel is now surrounded by hostile forces that previously had been neutralized by either an alliance or a peace treaty. And it was that neutralization that prevented a big war from breaking out in the region. As a result, Israel would only have to fight small wars since 1973. But the elimination of the threat of another major war changed during President Obama's first term. As the Israeli picture has changed vastly for the worse, it has done so through a series of events unfolding one after another. Consider the litany of events.

On first glance it is difficult to determine which has been worse for Israel, the shift of long-time ally Turkey against them, or the shift of Egypt from the status of peace partner to hostile neighbor again. Long term it is probably Turkey that plays out much more dangerously for Israel than Egypt. This is because it has the potential of uniting under its wings the newly Islamist nations borne from the so-called "Arab Spring," including Egypt, Tunisia, and Libya. If the rebels win in Syria, that nation will have become ripe as well. And a united Muslim front against Israel is the greatest danger it can possibly face. But the Egyptian situation is more immediate.

The "Arab Spring" has tilled fertile ground for the re-creation of Turkey's old Ottoman Empire, or, caliphate. Why is this so? Because it was strong dictators like Mubarak in Egypt that would never agree to submit under the tutelage of Turkey. It was the same with the dictators running places like Tunisia, Libya, and Syria. However, the main goal of those taking power from the dictators is a revived Muslim caliphate. And it is the Muslim Brotherhood now in control of Egypt that has been the driving force behind that goal throughout the entire region.[1] It seeks a Muslim caliphate and will cooperate with any authority it believes is associated with that goal. This is why Turkey had a strategic interest in seeing Egypt and Libya fall to Islamists, and why it now hopes the Syrian dictator falls as well, because he too would probably be replaced with radical Islamists.[2] The reason why is because that is exactly who appear to make up the core of rebel forces opposing him. Once in place, those religious zealots will also be willing to come in common cause with other Islamists in the region. It is why the overthrow of the Libyan dictator was good for Turkey, because that nation is also now becoming a growing stronghold for Islamists. As each Mideast domino falls to radical Islamists, the possibility of Turkey reconstituting its caliphate grows. And with the reemergence of any form of united Muslim front in the Middle East, the likelihood of Israel surviving dims as such a caliphate adds new nations under its control.

Early in his administration, Obama would skip Israel and go to Turkey, cozying up to a regime that was in the process of ending decades of secular democracy, replacing it with an Islamist one. The sudden confidence within Turkey's Islamist circles to make the move, again, occurred early in Mr. Obama's first term in office. Obviously, for some reason they were suddenly confident in their ability to crack down on the only safeguard preventing the rise of an Islamist government: the military. And the Obama administration would be silent as Turkey quietly rounded up 300 top military officers who were blocking the Islamist pathway.[3] The result of this action was that Turkey has, essentially, gone the way of Egypt, but having done so under the radar. As a former ally of Israel, it was another catastrophe for the tiny Jewish state, radically altering its security picture to the negative.

In the case of both Turkey and Egypt, strangely, and out of character, neither military of those countries attempted to resist as Islamist forces began making their move for control. That was strange, however, considering that within both nations the armed forces had been actively taking steps for decades to prevent such a shift in their countries. Since both militaries receive significant training and military hardware from the United States, and have for several decades, the United States has great sway within the upper ranks of the armed forces in both nations.[4] They are heavily dependent on the U.S. for spare parts, new equipment, training, and financial aid. As such, the question arises as to why, suddenly, did both militaries stand down as the shift toward Islamist regimes took place in their respective countries?

There is little doubt that had the United States made it clear to the military in Turkey to prevent that nation from slipping into the Islamist column, it would have taken whatever action necessary to protect the secular democracy. Essentially, it would have done what it had done since 1924 and Turkey would have remained out of the Islamist column.[5] This is a reasonable assumption considering they had taken such steps for decades. And it is the same in the case of Egypt. There too with the military so dependent on the United States, if a clear signal had been sent to them to support the embattled Mubarak regime, there is little doubt the Islamists in control there today would not have taken over the country. What is interesting is that neither military acted to its previous character, the character both exhibited prior to the rise of the Obama Administration. So it is reasonable to conclude that the Obama Administration did something that led the militaries of both nations to suddenly stand down, no longer blocking the ascendency of Islamists governments.

It is under President Obama, and his Secretary of State, Hillary Clinton, that this serious turn of events has transpired leaving Israel in a vastly more isolated position and more reliant on the United States by the year. But the move of Turkey away from a secular democracy toward an Islamist one is terrible for Western interests as well. As difficult as the West has found Islam to deal with in its fractured condition across the region, imagine having to deal with a greater and united Islam. The president's policies appear to be exactly what the current Islamist government in Turkey wanted. And with President Obama bragging on how close he is to the Turkish leader, Recip Erdogan, serious questions arise as to what advice President Obama has been taking to determine his policy in the Middle East.[6,7,8] But there would be a host of other signals by the U.S. president early in his term, leaving no doubt that "change" had made its way to the United States policy in the Mideast.

As mentioned previously, after delivering his big speech in Egypt at the start of his administration, he would send a message to every Muslim in the region by not visiting Israel, even though he would almost be on their doorstep. And the message was clear, indicating that this American president was not aligned with Israel as others had been. There is little doubt the message was clearly received across the region. But more messages of that type would be sent. On one occasion when the Israeli Prime Minister visited the White House, he was escorted to the back door, an entrance usually reserved for unsavory characters the U.S. seeks not to honor.[9] That too would be seen and, no doubt, discussed by Muslim leaders across the world. In addition to this new approach to the security of tiny Israel, other Obama Administration actions would increase pressure on Israel.

Historically speaking, there appears to be a direct relationship between a nation going to war and the feeling that it is being threatened. That is to say that in the case of Israel, as a threat grows so does the likelihood that they will attack whomever is threatening them. Now look at what has transpired with Iran since President Obama took office.

Since taking office the president has held back the sword of Israel from striking the advancing Iranian nuclear program, even as it appears to be approaching a point of invulnerability against attack. In a dramatic speech before the United Nations, the Israeli Prime Minister, Benjamin Netanyahu, reminded the world body of its stark responsibility to stop Iran from becoming a nuclear power. And for the first time Israel drew a red line for the world to see. In this case, literally the line was drawn by the prime minister on a poster board that contained a large bomb. It indicated that although Iran was close to attaining their goal, they had not yet crossed the point of no return. The speech was delivered in September of 2012, and the red line was indicated to be sometime in the summer of 2013.[10]

But there is something else that appears certain in the entire Iranian affair. As its nuclear program continues to grow, two Israeli calculations for war begin to change. First, the need on the part of Israel to attack grows as their enemy approaches the finish line of being able to produce nuclear weapons. Secondly, as the Iranians secure the main elements of their nuclear program deep under mountains, the Israeli ability to deal with it diminishes. Therefore, as time passes, and the threat grows, the ability to deal with it diminishes. As this all occurs, the need for the United States' vastly more powerful arsenal to help deal a death blow to the Iranian program grows. If enough time passes, it may become possible only for the United States to effectively deal with it, thus, granting President Obama even more leverage over the Israelis.

Also what must be factored into the threat equation for Israel is the change in status of both Turkey and Egypt. As bad as the Iranian threat is for Israel in and of itself, when combined with the shifting of Turkey from secular ally to Islamist opponent and Egypt from neutral to enemy once again, it has to be placed in an even more ominous light. With Israeli leadership fully aware of the growing constellation of security issues in the region since the rise of Barack Obama, a nuclear armed Iran has to be all the more unacceptable.

After a period of time, headlines in various publications would sum up how many Mideast observers saw the president's approach to Israel in his first term, and no doubt many in leadership positions within Israel must agree. Former New York City mayor, Ed Koch, a Jew and an Obama supporter, would write an article appropriately titled, "Obama's Hostility to Israel Continues."[11] In *The Washington Post*, conservative syndicated writer Charles Krauthammer looked at the president's "peace" proposal delivered in May 2011 and wrote an article titled, "What Obama did to Israel."[12] Later that month in *The Wall Street Journal*, an article written by Bret Stephens used a title that would embody the thoughts of many when considering the array of disasters that befell Israel during the Obama Administration, "An Anti-Israel President."[13]

But having secured within the minds of many the notion that he was not sympathetic to Israel during his first term, fear among Israel supporters of what a second term might be like was becoming the norm. The reasoning was something like this. If the president was willing to act so detrimentally against Israel during his first term, knowing he needed Jewish support to win a second term, in such a second term what would there be to restrain him from going even further against Israel? However, something strange began unfolding early in the second term that surprised many observers.

With the exception of choosing as his new Secretary of Defense Chuck Hagel, the president has engaged in a surprising about-face relating to Israel and her Prime Minister, Benjamin Netanyahu. And the headline in the March 2013 edition of *The New Yorker* magazine would say it all: "Why is Obama Being So Friendly to Netanyahu?"[14] The justification for that speculation would come from a series of surprising actions early in his second term. The president would suddenly decide to visit Israel, something he did not do in his entire first term surprising many Middle East observers. In line with that visit the following excerpt from *The New Yorker* article would voice what many were thinking and wondering as a result of this about-face.

> By far the most interesting question about the visit will be discussed, if at all, only behind closed doors: <u>What is Obama really up to?</u> Is he merely fulfilling one of the periodic obligations of his job-visiting a close ally —- and <u>playing to the Israeli lobby</u>? Or is this trip a precursor to something more serious: a determined effort to <u>restart the peace process and achieve a two-state solution before it is too late?</u>[15] (Emphasis added)

Even *The New Yorker* magazine, a liberal stalwart completely supportive of the president, would speculate on the motives behind the sudden shift in the administration's approach to Israel. And the trip does, indeed, raise the question, "What is Obama really up to?" In fact, the speculation that it was designed for "playing to the Israeli lobby ... in an effort to restart the peace process" would appear to be the most logical explanation.

But that visit would not be the only positive change Israel would see coming from Mr. Obama. Not long after the president's trip to Israel, the

United States would announce a $10 billion sale of sophisticated weapons to allies in the region, with Israel foremost to benefit from the sale. As mentioned previously, the package would include refueling aircraft necessary for extending the Israeli ability to attack long distances. And the most obvious target of such an attack would likely be Iran. The CBS News Internet headline would state: "Hagel announces new U.S. arms sales to Israel amid fears over possible war with Iran." (another rumor of war). Then when asked by a reporter how advisable it was to supply such a bounty of arms to Israel, enabling them to better attack Iran, the new Defense Secretary would indicate that such a "calculation has to be made by" Israel.[16] He would also point out that "Israel is a sovereign nation; every sovereign nation has a right to defend itself." It was noted how in the past the Obama Administration had always urged a diplomatic approach to the issue first, stating only that the military option was also on the table, but not this time. And this difference was picked up on by the CBS reporter, noting that this was a "softer approach than the U.S. has taken in the recent past" relating to an Israeli attack on Iran. Interestingly, the urge to give diplomacy more time was not included in the Secretary's statement.

The secretary would make other statements, telegraphing a potential shift in the U.S. effort to restrain Israel from attacking. Stating,

> Iran presents a threat in its nuclear program and Israel will make the decisions that Israel must make to protect itself and defend itself.[18]

One headline following the visit indicated that, effectively, the Secretary of Defense had given Israel a green light for an attack on Iran as well as against any Syrian efforts to move sophisticated weapons to its ally in Lebanon, Hezbollah.[19] Shortly after the visit, Israel enforced the red line concerning Syria and Hezbollah with a number of airstrikes against convoys carrying new and more powerful weapons into Lebanon. This action of attacking the Iranian ally, Syria, would ratchet up tension even more. But the message could not have been lost on Iran that Israel backs up its "red lines." And in Iran, near its capital of Tehran, a reporter for the BBC would report hearing explosions near an arms plant located there. Was it another Israeli covert attack as a prelude to war? If so, nobody was talking except about the rumor.

* * * * *

The sudden shift toward Israel in the beginning of the president's second term appears dedicated to creating a form of political capital as it relates to Israel. Which raises the question of why? Typically, the gathering of political capital is in order to spend it. And since he is already reelected, then it cannot be used to secure more Jewish support for his next election effort. It has to be for some other goal since domestic Jewish support is no longer needed for electoral reasons. And the only other goal that can logically be deducted is that this newly acquired political capital will, eventually, be used to press peace terms on Israel that will be difficult for many to accept. After having reassured the Muslim leaders in the region by already proposing peace terms at the U.N. that were almost everything they wanted, he can now safely shift his effort to his Jewish supporters in the U.S. in an effort to keep them in his camp when the hammer finally comes down on Israel.

* * * * *

If the "rumors" of war in verse 6 in the Book of Matthew relates to Israel, then, surely, it must relate to the endless "rumors" of an Israeli- Iranian war. The most likely way such a war would finally begin would be if Israel launches an attack against its nuclear program. And such an attack would just as surely usher in a full-blown war between the two nations.

93

THE COMING MIDEAST WAR AND PEACE TREATY

As reason dictates, the only thing that can end "rumors" of war is actual war. And to end the "rumors" it is necessary for the nation that has been rumored would attack, to finally do it.

If, indeed, war between Israel and Iran is approaching it will likely unfold sometime in the year 2013 or 2014. The case as to why that time frame is so important is multifold. Most importantly, never before has Israel drawn a clear red line in terms of a time frame for dealing with the growing Iranian nuclear threat. But it did so in September 2012. That announcement was made before the entire world at the United Nations. As a tiny, but militarily strong nation, in a very dangerous neighborhood, Israel placed its credibility on the line the day it drew that dramatic line before the world. The time frame offered by Prime Minister Netanyahu was the summer of 2013. There is, however, a real possibility that the time frame given before the U.N. was slightly earlier than it is in reality, in order to allow some flexibility for Israel. Also, since the Iranians were watching as the red line was being drawn, by providing an early time frame it can cause them to reach their maximum level of military alert, perhaps, too far in advance. This is speculation, of course, but it seems to make sense.

But there was something else that occurred during Netanyahu's United Nations speech warning the world that Israel had finally reached the end of the line in dealing with the Iranian threat. By starkly delivering such a deadline, he began laying the groundwork for creating diplomatic cover for the massive fallout expected from war between the two nations. Israeli credibility in drawing red lines would be a stark reminder to any who heard its warning issued at the United Nations that the threat of war was now quite real, bringing rumors to a new level.

The Israelis also drew a red line as it pertains to Syria, and made good on it by attacking Syrian convoys several times that were attempting to violate it. The red line here was directed at the transfer of more powerful weapons from Syria to Israel's enemy in Lebanon to the north, the terrorist militia Hezbollah. That heightened readiness to attack when its red lines are crossed demonstrates just that, a readiness for war and an absolute willingness to back up its red lines.[20] Interestingly, it should be noted that it took about ten years of "rumors" of war before Israel actually drew a red line concerning the Iranian nuclear program. Considering the Israeli willingness to enforce such red lines, the decision to place one out there for the entire world to see, and relating to a major power like Iran, had to take significant courage on the part of the Jews. That should be an ominous sign to Iran that the time of "rumors" of war with the Israelites is drawing to a close.

It is also apparent that the Iranian nuclear program is advancing by greater and greater leaps forward. A CBS online article in April 2013 indicated that various diplomats have warned that Iran has stepped up the installation of advanced uranium enrichment centrifuges.[21] And this move, it indicated, has tripled their installation of high-tech machines dedicated to the enrichment process. As a result, the time frame for Iran to reach the point of no return on their nuclear program has been dramatically reduced. This, obviously, is a development Israeli war planners are quite aware of.

There is also the case that as Israeli isolation in the region grows, so too, will its desire to prevent a new threat on the level of a nuclear armed Iran to exist. It just cannot allow another serious threat to its existence to reach fruition while it can still prevent it.

*   *   *   *   *

Besides political considerations, there is something else that should be looked at here as well, and that is heavenly signs. As shown in the chapter titled, "Signs in the Heavens," major events relating to the Jews have happened when a "tetrad" has appeared. One marked the death of

Jesus in 32-33 A.D. The next four tetrads after 33 A.D. appeared at times when the Jews were scattered and clear records are difficult to come by. However, those four tetrads appear to coincide with a terrible plague in Europe in the year 165 A.D., Charlemagne's defeat of Islam in 795-800 A.D., the Muslims sacking of Rome in 846 A.D., and the tetrad in 860-861 A.D. coincided with tumultuous times for both Christians and Jews at the hands of Muslim Crusaders.[22]

After the tetrad in 860-861 A.D., the next one was not until several centuries later, a time when it becomes easier to track big Jewish events. The expulsion of the Jews from Spain was marked with a tetrad that appeared in 1493-94. The next tetrad would not appear for another 455 years, but would arrive just in time in 1949-50 and represent a heavenly billboard marking the reestablishment of Israel in the land. However, the next arrived very quickly, in only 17 years and just in time to mark the reuniting of Holy Jerusalem under the control of Israel, again for the first time in almost 2,000 years. Now another tetrad is approaching for the years 2014 and 2015. Considering this major prophetic billboard in the heavens that approaches, it begs the question of what it is alerting mankind to look for. And considering that the last three tetrads took place when records relating to the Jews allow us to connect them each to a major event, should not the one approaching in 2014 and 2015 do the same? We also know that the one in 32-33 A.D. greatly impacted them as well, marking the death of Jesus. So this would appear to make it likely that whatever event will unfold, the Jews will be at the center of it all which now means the nation of Israel. This appears to gain credibility if such an Israel-Iran war would end a significant biblical time frame, which, in this case, would represent the conclusion of "but the end is not yet" in Matthew 24:6. It is reasonable to think that such a biblical milestone would be announced in the heavens, just as the taking of East Jerusalem in 1967 marked the end of the time that the Gentiles trodden it down. Remember, there was a tetrad in 1967-1968 marking the end of that biblical time frame.

Should the coming tetrad be warning of a regional war between Israel and Iran, the consequences of such a war would not only impact the region, but plunge the world into a crisis as well. With over 20% of the world oil traveling through the narrow Strait of Hormuz, located next to the Iranian coast, it is likely that the moment an attack begins, the Iranian military will begin unleashing a series of weapons dedicated to closing the strategic waterway. Part of the effort could involve the sinking of giant oil tankers in the waterway, in an effort to block the passage of tankers bringing their millions of barrels of crude oil to destinations across the globe.[23] But that would only be for starters.

The Iranian navy has been designed to assault larger ships, such as those in the U.S. Navy, with a swarm of small and swift attack boats armed with surface-to-surface missiles. War games including these kinds of attacks indicate they would meet with some success, thus hindering the ability of Western powers to reopen the waterway, for a period of time. Additionally, Iran has built a large supply of mines that could be released into the waterway causing shipping to come to a standstill while they are being cleared. However, as the clearing process takes place, it will be hindered by Iranian attacks against the ships involved in the operation. War games indicate the possibility of the Iranian tactics sinking major U.S. Navy vessels, like an aircraft carrier. If that did occur, it would bring shock to the American people and the West in general. It could also embolden radicals throughout the region.[24]

As a result, it is likely that for a period of time ranging from a week until, perhaps, a month, 20% of the world's oil supply might stop flowing, causing gasoline prices to skyrocket, along with the price of crude oil. Such a price spike would, undoubtedly, cause much economic hardship across the entire world, slowing down economies and bringing unemployment with it.[25] But that is only one potential response on the part of the Iranians.

With the U.S. southern border wide open to illegal crossings, and many of those crossing being OTMs, other than Mexicans, it is likely that Iran has a number of sleeper cells within the United States. Under the scenario of an attack against Iranian nuclear facilities, those cells would probably be awakened, resulting in a rash of terrorist attacks against U.S. targets. Former White House counter-terrorism official, Richard Clarke, believes that, "If we, the United States, were bombing Iran, then I think they'd certainly want to try to do something on our homeland because we were bombing their homeland." However, Iranian leaders have made it clear that any attack by Israel will be viewed as an attack by the United States. And in a conflict involving Israel, an American ally, and with the flow of oil through the Persian Gulf a strategic interest to the West, it is easy to see how the United States could get involved.[26]

It is also likely that Hezbollah, in Lebanon, and Hamas, in Gaza, acting as Iranian proxies, would begin fighting with Israel as well. With the spreading of fighting across Israel's borders, it opens the possibility that other regional players would be drawn into the conflict.[27]

It is also likely that an Israeli attack on Iran would set off the world's first cyber war. Just before striking Iran, Israel would attempt to blind their air defenses through a cyber attack. This attack would certainly be returned against Israel, and, depending on the circumstances, the West. Typically, attacks to blind an enemy's defenses would involve attacks against their energy grid, and the U.S. is very good at that. As a result, the Iranians would actively attempt to return the favor, and it would probably not be limited to Israel, but, again, the West in general. Any success on their part would cause great disruptions to the daily operations of Western economies at a time when gasoline prices would be skyrocketing.[28]

At the beginning of any attack by Israel, an immediate attack by Iran against Israeli cities with their long-range rockets would begin. Although not highly accurate, the combination of their numbers, as well as their high explosives, would result in a growing number of Israeli civilian casualties. Additionally, on Israel's northern border, Hezbollah, which possesses approximately 10,000 rockets aimed at Israel, may enter the war, sending an almost unending barrage of them into civilian targets.[29]

From the perspective of all participants, directly or indirectly involved, a war between Israel and Iran has the real potential of generating a worldwide crisis. The casualties will not only be Israeli and Iranian military and civilian personnel, but potentially the world economy impacting every person on the Earth. And the images of military action taking place on so widespread a scale would dominate the attention of the world for probably months. If terrorist attacks take place within Western nations as a result of such a war, a new dimension of fear would be added to the mix and on a worldwide scale. Any cyber attacks that succeeded in shutting down Western systems would add their unpleasant reality to sky-high gasoline prices that would already exit. Such a scenario would represent a worldwide crisis of the first order.

Within the confines of such a regional war, the potential for more outside players to get involved would exist, raising the possibility of nations such as Russia, an ally of Iran, feeling the need to lend its support to the embattled regime or lose face. China, a growing world power and highly dependent on oil from the Middle East, would have a real interest in seeing the war come to a quick conclusion.

During such an upheaval, diplomats and politicians would speculate and pontificate on how it all came about, and many would, no doubt, look at the Arab-Israeli conflict as the root of the issue. Even though from the Iranian perspective, the existence of Israel is the real issue, requiring a nuclear program to resolve it. Although such sentiments, combined with the drive to become a nuclear power would be the real reason for the conflict, the world, which did not respond while there was still time to act, will deny it. Instead of acknowledging that truth, which would infer culpability on them for having not acted, they will hearken back to the mantra that a resolution to the Arab-Israeli conflict is really the solution to the region's conflicts.

CHAPTER EIGHT

Never Waste a Crisis

A war between Israel and Iran would be a great crisis for the world, its impact reaching to the four corners of the globe. But according to some people, a crisis is a terrible thing to waste. The history of political leaders exploiting a crisis to achieve some goal is a long one. Often a crisis will be used to bring a nation into a war that during normal times could not happen. At least four U.S. wars since the year 1898 would originate from a crisis. Here is the gist of what happened in three of them. The common denomination in all is that each was used to bring about actions that previous to the crisis could not politically be accomplished. There is no historical judgment being made here on these events.

The Spanish American War

As the U.S.S. *Maine* sat in Havana harbor on the evening of January 15, 1898, none of its crew knew they were about to make history. At about 9:40 p.m. an explosion rocked the fighting ship. Whatever caused that initial explosion would be speculated on in the ensuing years. But soon it didn't matter. As the fire caused by the first explosion made its way to the ship's magazine, the massive 5-ton powder charges for its 10-inch guns began igniting. And once that began, it was the end of the U.S.S. *Maine* and more than 260 of her sailors who had been sleeping below deck when the tragedy began. As news of the sinking reached the states, the eyes of people turned to the Spanish military that ruled Cuba and was currently fighting against an insurgency on the island. But even before all the facts were known, newspapers like *The New York Journal* would release headlines that stirred up war tension between Spain and the United States.[1]

"CRISIS IS AT HAND...SPANISH TREACHERY."

The effort to use the crisis began quickly. Even though the president at the time, William McKinley, was against a war with Spain over the incident, soon politicians in the Congress would whip up public opinion to such an extent the president had little choice. Chants such as "Remember the Maine! To hell with Spain!" resounded across the nation. As a result, the "crisis" brought America to war against Spain. And in the years that followed, serious issues would be raised, questioning the likelihood of Spanish involvement in the sinking. But by that time it didn't matter. The interesting thing about it all was that Spain had a very strong interest in NOT mixing it up with the United States, because that would undermine their efforts against the insurgents. In fact, getting the United States into the mess was the only realistic way the insurgents could possibly win.[2] But in spite of the obvious, emotions were whipped up in another direction. And once emotion takes over, logic begins to recede.

Vietnam

Another "crisis" would be used to bring America to war in Vietnam, when in 1964 it would be reported that North Vietnamese vessels had attacked the U.S.S. *Maddox* in the Gulf of Tonkin. Soon war fever in Congress would result in the infamous "Gulf of Tonkin Resolution," which enabled President Johnson to take whatever action he saw fit against the Vietnamese Communists. And he saw fit to station about a half million troops there in the following years. It had been the "crisis" of the Gulf of Tonkin attack that enabled the dramatic action.[3] Here too there would be questions as to the reality and extent of the attack.

Iraq

After the attacks of September 11, 2001, the United States would go to war in Afghanistan, where it had become clear the perpetrators of the dastardly assault were stationed. When the government of that backward nation indicated no willingness to bring the likely perpetrators, al-Qaeda, to justice, the United States began an offensive to end that nation as a safe haven for terrorism. However, although the connection of Afghanistan to al-Qaeda was clear, political elements within the United States pushed to include Iraq as a target, and eventually, the U.S. went to war there also. And it was the atmosphere of the September 11th crisis which enabled that second military move.[4]

Within the conditions of a crisis, things can get done that previously were impossible to achieve. During the administration of President Franklin Roosevelt, the body of legislation representing his "New Deal" solution to the Great Depression would have never gotten through Congress without that crisis.[5] When people are crying out for a solution to some great issue of the moment, anything that can be packaged as that solution will be viewed with favor. This appears to be true, even if it does not solve the problem. For all of Roosevelt's New Deal legislation that was enacted, many economic historians appear to agree that it was only the onset of World War II that finally brought the United States out of the Great Depression.[6] Nonetheless, the legislation was packaged as a solution to the crisis and, thus, garnered the public's support.

Simply taking action in the midst of a crisis gives the public a sense that something is being done to fix it, even if it is the wrong thing. This is because within the public there is only a small segment of individuals who truly seek to obtain a depth of understanding on major events. As a result of this, a crisis can be used to enact the goals of those in charge, goals that previously were impossible to achieve. And current-day political leaders would openly embrace this notion, having finally figured out a path to their goals, even if the solution is questionable.

President Obama's Secretary of State, Hillary Clinton, would openly talk about the positive nature of a crisis before her European counterparts in 2009, as the global financial meltdown was still going full bore. Her statement of encouragement to those present was to "Never waste a good crisis ... Don't waste it when it can have a very positive impact on climate change and energy security."[7] And for those whose policy goals include a highly unpopular carbon tax, touted to be a solution to "climate change," that period of economic turmoil presented an opportunity to get it passed under the guise that it would somehow help the nation come out of the financial crisis. The new global tax was presented as a solution, even though new taxes during an economic crisis appear to have a negative economic impact.[8] And since the crisis was worldwide, and so would be that new tax, it would be especially negative. But, nonetheless, the crisis was an opportunity to not be taken lightly by those with goals to achieve.

The president's Chief of Staff, Rahm Emanuel, would echo Ms. Clinton's sentiments, pointing out to a reporter from *The New York Times* that

"Rule 1: Never let a crisis go to waste," because "They are opportunities to do big things."[9] And their boss, President Obama, chimed in during a Saturday radio address that there "is great opportunity" in the midst of the "great crisis" befalling America.[10]

In the months after the 2008 presidential election, notable newspapers such as *The Wall Street Journal* observed that with the nation in the midst of a major financial and economic crisis, it presented some real challenges for the incoming president.[11] But it also observed how within such an atmosphere of a crisis there were present many opportunities for the administration to drive through their agenda. It had been just prior to this article being published that Obama's future chief of staff, Rahm Emanuel, had made his increasingly infamous remark that the crisis presented an opportunity. And it would not take long for the new administration to begin implementing that philosophy in crisis management.

The president would immediately begin pushing for a "stimulus" package of legislation being touted by its supporters as a safeguard from an extended recession, as well as protection for the banking system. However, as components of the bill began to form, it became apparent that it was becoming one of the largest pieces of pork legislation in history. And in the final version of the $819 billion bill, so much pork had been stuffed into it that not one Republican voted for it.[12] Yet, in spite of what the bill represented, the president threatened that if it was not passed it would develop the "Crisis into a catastrophe." In describing what would happen if the bill did not pass, the president painted a stark picture saying that ...

> Millions more jobs will be lost. More businesses will be shuttered. More dreams will be deferred.[13]

And with more than enough votes within his party, the president won a resounding victory through the atmosphere of a crisis. The president continued to exploit a crisis in order to gain political leverage over his opponents. As oil prices rose to dizzying heights, the president would

105

push for the highly unpopular "cap and trade," a tax dedicated to the "climate change" crisis.[14] However, the connection between the oil problem and "cap and trade" was so dubious that enough members of his own party opposed it, making it impossible to pass. But it was the atmosphere of a crisis that the president sought to use to achieve his goal.

During the health care legislation debate, the massive 2,700-page bill was withheld from members of Congress until the last moment, with, then Speaker of the House, Nancy Pelosi, urging them to vote in favor of it so they could finally see what was inside it.[15] The inference was that the crisis was so great that there was not enough time to spend reading it. And it passed.

Later in his administration when a stunningly tragic mass shooting of children at Sandy Hook Elementary School took place, the president would use the grief in its aftermath to seek passage of legislation restricting various gun rights.[16] However, many would question how the proposed legislation would prevent madmen from carrying out such dastardly deeds in the future. But, nonetheless, the crisis was utilized to advance a previously desired agenda.

It is obvious that the Obama Administration is one that seeks to use a crisis to advance its agenda. We know this because it has done so repeatedly since coming into office. Therefore, it is reasonable to believe it will do so again. Such an approach to getting what it wants appears to be in the DNA of its top officials. And it is also clear that the solutions offered to resolve a crisis often do not address the problem. Because these traits have been demonstrated as well, they too should be present in the way a future crisis is handled. And this finally leads us to the volatile Middle East.

Should war in the Middle East erupt between Israel and Iran, either from a direct Israeli attack, or as a result of some other spark, the world will possibly enter a phase of crisis not seen in years. And in light of Israel finally drawing a red line in the region, it is clear that such a crisis could happen at any time, probably in 2013 or 2014. It would appear doubtful it could extend beyond that time frame, however, because if it does, Israel will lose credibility when it speaks to its many enemies. Such a consequence would have dire consequences for the tiny Jewish state, emboldening the multitude of enemies surrounding it.

Within the crisis associated with such a war the first order of international diplomacy would be to stop it. However, once a war begins, that is often very difficult to do. In the case of a war between Israel and Iran, wherein Israel attacked, the need on the Israeli part to complete the task of destroying or, greatly setting back the Iranian nuclear program would be paramount. It is difficult to imagine that they would be willing to attack and thus cause the great furor such an attack would engender, and not seek to finish the objective. That means that from the Israeli perspective, the necessity of multiple attacks over the course of, perhaps, several weeks would be needed.

On the part of Iran, it would be dedicated to extracting every ounce of the pound of flesh from Israel that it could with punishing rocket attacks directed against its cities. And the Western nations would also become likely targets of Iranian wrath. So it too would be hesitant to stop before it felt enough harm had been done to Israel and the West.

With such attacks going back and forth, and potentially terrorist attacks taking place within Western nations, blame would begin being directed against the one that attacked first, which, probably would be Israel. If Israel is the one to attack first, which appears likely, it would begin to experience great anger across European nations directed at its embassies and citizens. And as gasoline prices surge higher, it would only fuel that anger. One such example of this European response took place as Israeli forces entered Gaza to stop continuous rocket attacks against their civilian population. Even though the "incursion" was an effort at self-defense, the response in Europe was negative toward Israel. There was even a rash of anti-Semitic acts here and there. But that muted response came from a conflict that did not impact the average citizen in Europe. However, in any regional war between Israel and Iran, the impact could be great resulting in a dramatic increase in anti-Israel activities.

As the war would progress, pressure on the United States would likely grow to the point where it would, inevitably, need to get involved. And if the United States did get involved, it would be the one that would have to finish it. That will not please many within the U.S. who have had their fill of wars in the Middle East. Adding to that angst will be if successful terrorist attacks occur in America, making the average citizen fully aware of how a conflict in a far-away part of the world impacted them. Such awareness can easily be morphed by talented politicians into a concept. And in this scenario the concept will likely be that the root of the Mideast problems are the Israeli-Palestinian conflict. And after all is said and done that is probably the conclusion that the masses will be directed toward. Under the conditions of such a crisis, a number of things become possible. First, it is possible to direct the masses as well as the intelligentsia of Western nations to the belief that a resolution of the Israel-Palestinian conflict will prevent such wars from taking place again in the future. And it will certainly be pointed out the likelihood of another one in the following years if something is not done to resolve it permanently. But there is a problem with such a solution being a real one, and it would be summed up by a leading "moderate" Palestinian leader in May 2013.

The land claimed by the Palestinians can be divided into two separate parts. There is Gaza, ruled by the terrorist organization Hamas, and the "West Bank," ruled by the Palestinian Authority (PA). It is the PA where Western hopes for a future peace settlement of the conflict rest because of the belief in some quarters that its leadership has some moderate elements within it. In this case, the term "moderate" means willing to talk and negotiate with Israel, along with a willingness to verbally acknowledge the Jewish state's right to exist. However, within the "moderate" PA, grammar school children are taught that a good Jew is a dead one. In Gaza, although children are taught this same thing, Hamas will not verbally acknowledge the right of the Jewish state to exist and, thus, are considered not moderate.

There is also the tendency for PA ruling members when speaking to Western press to sound reasonable and willing to accept Israel. But when speaking to Arabic media, they display a willingness to speak in a way that would shock Western sensitivities by expressing their true thoughts to their brother Muslims. One of them, Jibril Rajoub, a senior Palestinian Authority official, and frequently characterized as "moderate," would well demonstrate this practice. While speaking to Lebanon's Al Mayadeen TV, and speaking in Arabic, he would reveal the true thoughts of those the world seeks to have Israel negotiate with.

After the interviewer referred to any peace talks with Israel as "the negotiation game," Rajoub would suggest that the PA only does that because they do not possess the military strength to overcome Israel by force at present.[17] His sentiments would echo other "moderate" PA officials' statements that they seek to avoid confrontation with Israel only because they are not yet strong enough to defeat them. Then, demonstrating the degree of PA hatred for the Israeli people in the same interview, Rajoub reassured the Al Mayadeen TV audience that, "I swear that if we had a nuke, we'd have used it this very morning."[18]

This mentality appears to be prevalent among those who represent the Palestinian people, effectively, making it impossible for any "peace agreement" between Israel and the Palestinian Authority, to represent a true peace and a true settlement of the conflict. So, although the world will force a settlement on the parties and call it "peace and safety," it will not be until hearts are changed. And no piece of paper can do that. But since such sentiments seeking Israel's destruction come from many quarters, the Iranian nuclear program takes on an even more ominous note.

If the Iranian drive to develop nuclear weapons is allowed to succeed, then the likelihood is that groups dedicated to the destruction of Israel will finally possess the means to accomplish the dark task. But in spite of that terrible and calculated threat of the Jews suffering yet another Holocaust, world leaders will not likely be sympathetic as a regional war burns between Israel and Iran.

Because reasoning is limited to those exercising it, under the conditions of a regional war crisis those leaders will be few and far between. The first order of business for world leaders in the aftermath of such a crisis will be to take some form of action that will reassure their populations that steps have been taken to solve the problem for the future. And in line with that, the more dramatic the action taken, the greater will be the appearance that they have done something to resolve it.

What will placate Western leaders, Russian, Chinese, and some Muslim leaders, as well as the world population, will be a peace agreement between Israel and the Palestinians. That is because many people believe that a settlement of that conflict will result in a host of Middle East problems beginning to fade. And many leaders have been pushing for a peace agreement along the lines presented by President Obama at the United Nations in May 2011.

After the crisis of a regional war between Israel and Iran, the stage will be set to force a "peace" agreement finally. And in this case it will be the entire world that will demand it.

CHAPTER NINE

A Treaty with Many

W ithin the context of the Israeli-Palestinian conflict, one event has taken place that transcends all others: The United Nations beginning to take action to resolve the dispute by unilaterally establishing a new nation, Palestine. It is that single fact which occurred in President Obama's first term that is the most ominous for Israel, even exceeding the turn of both Turkey and Egypt against her. The result has been to place the ultimate power to force a "peace" settlement outside Israel's control. And it was clearly the actions of the Obama Administration that led it to the U.N.

As discussed in the chapter, "Israel Surrounded," the Obama Administration would come under sharp criticism for effectively killing negotiations between the Israelis and Palestinians on two separate occasions. The first action was to inject a new condition for negotiations between the parties, thus, killing them before they could begin. Amazingly, it was the Obama Administration, not the Palestinian side, that injected the new demand. The second was when the president nearly tripped over his own shoelaces in May of 2011 to give his big Middle East speech to the United Nations the day before Netanyahu gave his.[1] The president used the opportunity to lay out his vision for Middle East peace first. However, there was a problem with his vision. It was radically out of step with previous U.S. policy to the dispute, closely resembling what the Palestinians' side had been seeking all along. And a multitude of the president's supporters would acknowledge that fact.

Considering that the plan was so radical that it killed any chance for negotiations to take place, in fact, for a second time, that move was very strange. Why wouldn't he wait for Netanyahu to present his plan and see if it offered anything new? His actions would cause even some of his allies to question his competency in doing this, noting its negative effect on chances for negotiations between the parties for the second time in his first term. The president's plan was so pro-Palestinian that the Israeli Prime Minister did not even bother to present his own plan, which he traveled halfway around the world to deliver before the world body.[2] And the world will never know what, if any, concessions would have been offered in it. However, the president was not incompetent, but brilliant, because this is what the effect his first term actions have produced.

By presenting a plan that was essentially what the Palestinians wanted and, thus, killing negotiations again, the parties to the dispute would remain miles apart before the world. And since there had not been any kind of negotiations of any consequence during his entire first term, it is that fact which caused the issue to make its way to the United Nations instead of the negotiating table with both parties talking.

As it pertains to Israel and the United Nations, there is this overriding fact: It is an organization where Israel is hopelessly outnumbered. Interestingly, at the negotiating table, Israel retained control over its future and was not outnumbered. Now, with no negotiations taking place, the

United Nations picked up the ball, seeking to create a Palestinian state, again, just as it created a Jewish one in 1948. But any current action taken to create a Palestinian state by the United Nations will be the second time it has attempted to do this because in 1948, along with Israel, it tried to establish a state for the Arabs in Palestine. However, instead of choosing their own state, the Palestinians decided to join the surrounding Arab nations in an effort to prevent the Jews from getting their state. In the process they not only lost that war, but their state as well.

Although the vast majority of members in the United Nations are overwhelmingly against Israel and pro-Palestine, creating such a state takes more than a simple majority or even super majority vote, of its members.[3] If that were the case, the Palestinians would have won it long ago. It is only the United Nations Security Council where the U.S. has the all-powerful veto power, where a new state can be created and approved. With the efforts to bring that new nation of Palestine into being through the U.N., the veto held by the United States to block it grows in importance. And the person who ultimately holds the power of that veto is Barack Obama. So, ironically, the president, who has killed negotiations between the parties, thus funneling it into the waiting hands of the United Nations, has the ability to say yea or nay about the matter. It is a form of control over Israel with an intense focusing of the power to force a "peace" settlement in the hands of a president whose administration has been a security disaster for the Jewish state.

All previous attempts for a negotiated settlement of the dispute between the Israelis and Palestinians have deeply involved the United States, and later, the Quartet. The Quartet, of course, consists of the United States, Russia, European Union, and the United Nations all acting as one to remove the lands from Israel in the name of peace. Realistically, however, without some great leverage over the Israelis, any future effort toward a "peace" settlement will get nowhere. Before Obama, the only leverage of great power over the Israelis that an American president possessed was the threat to stop financial and military aid to them. Although theoretically possible, from a practical/political standpoint it was impossible. Any such move would cause Congress to go into rebellion against the president who dared to do it, even members from within his own party. Effectively, the votes within Congress to override any such radical action against Israel would be there. Not only would that mean Israel would continue to receive the aid, but the president making the attempt would be politically wounded without any benefit derived. Therefore, realistically, it was never an option. And the same is true during the Obama Administration, rendering that method of forcing the Israelis into an agreement non-existent.

Considering that all parties to the dispute have been struggling to find a solution since 1991, and have reached a point of complete stalemate, if all things remain the same the prospect for any real advance toward a "peace" treaty are slim. It is the old adage that if you keep doing the same thing, you will continue to get the same results. And the same results in this case represent no treaty. In fact, both the Israelis and Palestinians have played the game for so long that they have become experts, after a fashion, at preventing any form of progress at the negotiating table for their own political reasons. And both parties have mastered the art of appearing sincere, while having no intention, whatsoever, of compromising on any issue of substance that would represent "progress," with the game going round and round. Regardless of what diplomatic words are spoken by either party to the dispute, the issue is unsolvable and the reasons why are simple.

For the Palestinians, East Jerusalem must be their future capital. For Israel, both East and West Jerusalem are their indivisible capital they will never agree to divide again. To understand their fervency in this regard, it is necessary to understand that they waited almost 2,000 years to reunite it. For the Palestinians, their new state must push Israel back to borders that existed prior to the 1967 war. For Israel, that would represent borders that invited aggression against them and would make them vulnerable to extinction. It would also require the removal of several hundred thousand settlers who now live in those areas. For the Palestinians, all refuges who were displaced since the 1948 war must be allowed to return to their previous homes... that's several million people! Such a move would effectively end the state of Israel by Muslims outnumbering them within their own country. For Israel, national suicide is not an option. Additionally, although the Israelis control East Jerusalem, it is the area of real estate called the Temple Mount located within it that contains holy shrines the Jews waited, again, 2,000 years to possess. It is very difficult to imagine that Israel will relinquish it again.[4] In conclusion, anyone who says the differences can be bridged is being unrealistic. To bridge such differences, a solution will have to be imposed by the world.

Today, however, with the dispute having been guided to the United Nations, the power now possessed by President Obama over Israel's future is almost absolute, but without nearly the political fallout of other options. At any point in time of the president's choosing, he can instruct the U.S. Ambassador to the U.N. to not veto a Palestinian statehood resolution. With such a threat able to be delivered to the Israelis privately, the pressure on them will be great to agree to terms they would never before have considered. And if they do not agree, and a Palestinian state is approved by the world community, the consequences for Israel will be cataclysmic, placing them in the position of occupying the territory of another U.N. member. Checkmate!

It would be under President Obama's administration, and no other, when the Palestinian Authority applied to the United Nations for assistance in establishing key governmental structures necessary for the granting of statehood by the world body. In its report dated March 2013, the

U.N. reiterated that the Palestinian Authority "was above the threshold for a functioning state in the key sectors studied."[5] In other words, it is only during the Obama Administration where the U.N. could approve a Palestinian state because the Palestinian Authority was deemed ready to become one. Within that same report, both parties to the conflict were urged to "respect their obligations" under the "roadmap."[6] This referred to the Quartet's "roadmap to peace" proposals that stipulated what steps both parties must take in order to settle their differences so the lands could be removed from Israel for the establishment of a Palestinian state. The report would go on to warn that although the elements for a functioning nation state were now in place, the political side of things was not yet ready.

It would also be within the Obama Administration, and no other, that the United Nations conferred a new upgraded status for the Palestinian Authority, that of non-member state status.[7] By doing this, the U.N. was saying that they are a state but not a member of the United Nations. And the Reuters News headline would say it all: "Palestinians win implicit U.N. recognition of sovereign state."[8] The votes counted in favor of this big step were a lopsided victory for them, with 138 nations voting in favor, and only nine against.[9] With Israel doing everything possible to prevent its passing, the vote represents how outnumbered they are as their vital interests have been shifted from the negotiating table to the United Nations. Checkmate again!

In line with that U.N. recognition, the Palestinian leader, Mahmoud Abbas, sought a division of the lands in question eerily similar to what President Obama supported within his big speech in May 2011. And the Palestinian drive for U.N. recognition all appeared to begin sometime after Mr. Abbas's meeting with president Obama in April, 2010. According to *Harretz* newspaper, following that meeting, Mr. Obama gave assurances to Mr. Abbas of a Palestinian state in the near future.[10] Strangely, the president felt comfortable giving such an assurance in spite of there not being any form of negotiations taking place. And even stranger, it was his actions that prevented them. There would also begin appearing other ominous signs early in 2013 coming from the president himself concerning a potential shift in U.S. diplomatic support for Israel.

Within Washington, D.C., there are certain journalists who appear favored by the White House during each administration. And as a result those administrations will use those journalists to become carriers of messages to the public which top administration officials want released, but do not want their names attached to it. One such journalist, Jeffrey Goldberg, has been used by the Obama Administration on several occasions to channel public messages to Israel and their prime minister on both the Iranian issue as well as the Palestinian dispute. And on a particular occasion it would be the Palestinian dispute that would bring Goldberg to the White House, chosen to carry an ominous message for the Israelis just after they suffered a serious defeat at the United Nations.

After making it clear that President Obama believes the Israeli prime minister "doesn't understand what Israel's best interests are," the officials added that the president believes Netanyahu is "a political coward, an essentially, unchallenged leader who nevertheless is unwilling to lend or spend political capital to advance the cause of compromise." As harsh as those words were, it was what Goldberg reported next that must have brought a chill up the spines of Israeli leaders. Discussing all the diplomatic cover the United States has been giving Israel at the United Nations, especially in the face of initiatives to create a Palestinian state, it was warned that Israel is likely to feel a significant change in that protection in the near future. Writing Goldberg, "Israel could well find itself even more isolated."[11]

With only nine other U.N. members voting against the U.N. initiative to award non-member state status to the Palestinian Authority, the inference was clear: The United States would no longer vote against efforts to create a Palestinian state by a U.N. vote. Such words would represent the form of a first warning shot to Israel with the message clear: "Play ball with what we want or else."

In line with administration tendencies to use a crisis atmosphere to accomplish the politically impossible, the new Secretary of State, John Kerry, appeared before the House Foreign Affairs Committee to carry on the tradition. After pointing out that there has been nearly no Israeli-Palestinian talks in the past four years, he added that no solution was in sight after more than six decades of conflict. Then he said something interesting, perhaps telegraphing administration intentions regarding the whole issue.

> I think we have some period of time <u>a year to a year-and-a-half to two years, or it's over.</u> Everybody I talk to in the region and all the supporters globally who care want us to move forward on a peace effort. They're all worried about timing here. So there's an urgency to this, in my mind, and I intend on behalf of the president's instructions to honor that urgency and see what we can do to move forward.[12] (Emphasis added)

When asked why he believed so little time was left for a two-state solution, especially in light of the fact that the conflict has been around for over six decades, Mr. Kerry would not say. But the tenor of his message was clear. There is currently no hope of resolving the conflict because the parties have not even been speaking to each other. And by stating that there are only two years left or it can never be done, a sense of urgency or crisis exists in the matter. Ironically, that limited do-or-die time frame happens to fall within the next two years, 2014 and 2015, during Obama's final term in office. But it is the effective killing of negotiations between the parties during the president's first term that placed the matter in the newly anointed status of a crisis.

In line with that approach, the Arab League, an organization of Arab states dedicated to furthering their common goals, made a historic concession in their previous proposals for peace between the Israelis and Palestinians. In those previous plans the demand that all lands not possessed by Israel prior to the 1967 Six-Day War be returned without any exception was their steadfast position, and one in which they had refused to depart from. That, however, presented a very big practical problem since several hundred thousand Israeli citizens had settled within that area. Moving them was not an option and so as long as that was the demand of the Arab side, the positions between the parties could not be reconciled. But in 2013, the Arab League came out with a more flexible proposal wherein land swaps would be acceptable with equal amounts of land transferred from other parts of Israel to make up for the land that had been settled in.[13] This now removes one major block from reaching a "peace" treaty.

Considering the litany of events and how they interact with one another, there has entered the hands of Barack Obama the instruments necessary to apply the ultimate amount of pressure on Israel when the time arrives. If it has been done wittingly, then it is a masterpiece beyond the bounds of the natural. But regardless, it has been masterfully accomplished even if it is yet hidden before its multiplicity unfolds. And its unfolding will probably occur sometime in 2014 or 2015.

From a purely Middle East peace perspective, without regard to any other geopolitical considerations, nothing like what has aligned has ever before been accomplished. With his discernible and surprising shift toward Israel in the early days of his second term, what appeared confusing, and even incompetent in his first term, to Middle East observers, is now is making sense.

CHAPTER TEN

The Sequence of Prophetic Events

T he key to unlocking a sequence of biblical prophetic events that appear on the verge of unfolding is found in the Book of Matthew,
chapter 24, verses 6 through 8. This was covered thoroughly in chapter 6,
"Wars and Rumors of Wars," and now will be connected to other Scripture, which will allow a sequence of prophetic events to unfold from it.
It is Jesus who is providing a rendition of what those alive at a time in the
future should be looking for. His detailed descriptions would famously
be referred to as the Olivet Discourse. As He sits on the Mount of Olives delivering it, these key verses appear quickly, only a few lines into
the prophetic chapter. However, herein we see why understanding it is
much easier today than in days past. There is a certain interpretation of
these three verses which perfectly fits the current geopolitical situation
and causes an array of other prophetic Scripture to begin fitting together
in what appears to be a form of true harmony. In fact, it appears to show
EXACTLY where mankind is at present in the prophetic narrative. And

once that reference point is established, it then provides the sequence of the next several events that unfold from there.

The following Scriptures will be referred to repeatedly in this chapter. They are: Matthew 24:6-8; 1 Thessalonians 5:1-3; Joel 2:30-32; Joel 3:1-2; and Luke 28:21:24-25. Each will be repeated during the course of this chapter to make various points. The following listing of them is provided here to show the interlocking harmony among them that this chapter is dedicated to demonstrating. However, it is Matthew 24:6-8 that is the key causing the rest to fit together in harmony with the others. (EACH OF THE FOLLOWING SCRIPTURES HAS A BRIEF COMMENT IN PARENTHESES AFTER IT.) **Also, the key words being focused on are in bold print.**

Matthew 24

6: And ye shall hear of **wars and rumours of wars**: (RESTORED ISRAEL WILL EXPERIENCE WARS AND NOTABLE RUMORS OF WARS)

see that ye be not troubled: for all these things must come to pass,

but the end is not yet. (BUT BIRTH PAINS HAVE NOT YET BEGUN)

7: For nation shall rise against nation, and kingdom against kingdom: (A GREAT WAR BETWEEN THE NATIONS)

and there shall be famines, and pestilences, (THE WAR BETWEEN THE NATIONS RESULTS IN NOTABLE FAMINES AND PESTILENCES ACROSS THE EARTH)

and earthquakes, in divers places. (NOTABLE EARTHQUAKE ACTIVITY WILL ALSO BEGIN TAKING PLACE)

8: All these are the beginning of sorrows. (NOW IT IS THE BEGINNNG OF BIRTH PAINS)

I Thessalonians 5

1: But of the times and the seasons, brethren, ye have no need that I write unto you.

2: For yourselves know perfectly that **the day of the Lord** so cometh as a thief in the night.

3: For when they shall say, Peace and safety; (PEACE TREATY BETWEEN ISRAEL AND PALESTINE)

then sudden destruction cometh upon them, (WAR BETWEEN THE NATIONS SUDDENLY BREAKS OUT)

as travail upon a woman with child; and they shall not escape. (IT'S THE BEGINNING OF BIRTH PAINS)

Joel 2

30: And I will shew wonders in the heavens and in the earth, (UNUSUAL HEAVENLY EVENTS TAKE PLACE)

blood, and fire, and pillars of smoke. (A NOTABLE WAR TAKES PLACE)

31: The sun shall be turned into darkness, and the moon into blood, (A SOLAR ECLIPSE AND BLOOD MOONS TETRAD)

before the great and terrible day of the Lᴏʀᴅ come. (THE ECLIPSE AND TETRAD OCCUR BEFORE THE BIRTH PAINS BEGIN)

32: And it shall come to pass, that whosoever shall call on the name of the LORD shall be delivered: for in mount Zion and in Jerusalem shall be deliverance, as the LORD hath said, and in the remnant whom the LORD shall call.

Joel 3

1: For, behold, in those days, and in that time, when I shall bring again the captivity of Judah and Jerusalem,

2: I will also gather all nations, and will bring them down into the valley of Jehoshaphat, and will plead with them there for my people and for my heritage Israel,

whom they have scattered among the nations, and parted my land. (THE NATIONS' PREVIOUS ACTION OF REMOVING THE LANDS FROM ISRAEL THROUGH THE PEACE TREATY HAS CAUSED SOME TO LEAVE ISRAEL AND THIS SCATTERING IS THE REASON FOR THIS WAR)

Luke 21

24: And they shall fall by the edge of the sword, and shall be led away captive into all nations: (JERUSALEM FALLS IN 70 A.D. TO THE ROMANS)

and Jerusalem shall be trodden down of the Gentiles, (THE GENTILES POSSESS IT UNTIL THEIR TIME IS UP)

until the times of the Gentiles be fulfilled. (IN JUNE 1967, THE JEWS REGAIN ALL OF JERUSALEM, ENDING THE "TIMES OF THE GENTILES" POSSESSING IT)

25: And there shall be signs in the sun, and in the moon, and in the stars; (THE NEXT TETRAD SINCE THE "TIMES OF THE GENTILES" ENDED IS 2014-2015)

and upon the earth distress of nations, with perplexity; (NATION RISING AGAINST NATION)

the sea and the waves roaring;

The Coming Israel-Iran War

Very early in Matthew 24, Jesus lays out what those living at a certain time in the future will observe concerning events relating to Israel as well as the world. He is describing a set of geopolitical circumstances that will begin to appear that will allow those with understanding to identify them as the beginning of His warnings. As mentioned in the chapter titled, "Wars and Rumors of Wars," the Scriptures in Matthew 24:6-8 are clearly divided into two separate biblical time frames. One is where "the end is not yet," and the other represents "the beginning of sorrows." So we know they are talking about two different events in which the reader goes from one biblical time frame of pre-birth pains in verse 6, into another, the much-feared birth pains phase that verse 7 ushers in. So the Scripture is telling us that each verse is referring to separate events since they are in different prophetic time frames. It is presented in this book that verse 6, "wars and rumors of wars," can only be talking about the condition of current-day Israel, and it is verse 7 that is referring to the nations across the Earth. Besides both verses representing completely different prophetic time frames, there are other reasons indicating this is the correct way to view these three verses. Here is a quick refresher.

The first indication that verse 6 is NOT referring to wars involving nations across the Earth is that it is indicated in the very next verse that "nation shall rise against nation." It is an obvious redundancy if verse 6 is also referring to nations across the Earth because verse 7 is specifically referring to nations across the Earth. How can verse 6 be referring to the nations across the Earth being at war when they must rise to go to war in the next verse? In other words, how can nations that have already risen to war in verse 6, rise to go to war in verse 7? In order for one to rise, one must not have already risen. The better interpretation is that verse 6 is referring to the condition of Israel, not the nations across the Earth, which are then handled in verse 7. And the following adds to why that interpretation makes more sense.

In addition to the clear redundancy in verses 6 and 7, there is this. As previously noted, it is only Israel since its founding that has experienced a war on average about every 4.6 years. And that condition represents a nation that has heard a lot about war since coming back into its Promised Land. Since we know the Bible is Israel centric, verse 6 renders us to have to choose between Israel and the nations across the Earth for its application. Additionally, it appears Jesus was speaking about the condition of Israel when He told the Jews listening to Him to look for "wars and rumors of wars," because in His next sentence, verse 7, He specifies the condition of the nations across the Earth saying clearly, "nation shall rise against nation." He also tells them that this observation represents the beginning of the birth pains ("these are the beginning of sorrows"). This makes it very clear that the "wars and rumors of wars" noted in verse 6 are separate and different from verse 7, because in verse 6 it is noted that "the end is not yet." Again, since the events in verse 6 exist in one prophetic time frame, and the events in verse 7 are in another, these two Scriptures cannot be referring to the same event. So not only is it the differing time frames involved here, but the fact that Israel today is the one that has been experiencing the condition described by verse 6 of wars. Since we are told in verse 7 that the nations across the Earth will rise to war against each other, then to be able to rise they must be quietly settled down in a state of relative peace as the "wars and rumors of wars" in verse 6 are being completed. And this is exactly the current geopolitical conditions.

As previously noted since its rebirth, Israel has existed in a condition of "wars" taking place on average every 4.6 years. Try to imagine that. And also consider that Israel is not a large country either geographically or in terms of population, so the impact of each war on its people has been all that much greater. Essentially, in many of those wars almost every able-bodied man or woman of age had to fight. So it would appear that of all the nations, it is Israel that fulfills the "wars" part of verse 6 better than any. Since we see that Israel has fulfilled this requirement so well since its founding in 1948, what about the "rumors" part in verse 6? For verse 6 to apply to Israel this too would need to be fulfilled.

It has been since the year 2003 that the world has been waiting for a war between Israel and Iran to break out at any time, and bring with it a regional disaster that is feared across the globe. Part of such a war would almost surely involve Lebanon's Hezbollah, and Gaza's Hamas, fighting on the side of Iran. Since that year, these "rumors of wars" between Israel and Iran have been as persistent as they have been frightening. They are the most persistent "rumors of wars" seen anytime within the twentieth century and currently stretching into a decade. This is so true that diligent and dedicated diplomatic efforts by the United Nations and various nations have been consistently engaged in to prevent the calamity of it all. In fact, efforts to appease Israel in the hope of keeping her sword sheathed have included significant "sanctions" designed to make life so miserable within Iran that they would give up on their nuclear ambitions. And the potential of this war has literally become a topic of constant speculation of when it will happen and how bad it will be, with each year looking like it will be the one in which it will take place. Therefore, of all the nations on the Earth, it is Israel since 2003 that has experienced the persistence of "rumors of wars" to a highly notable degree and, thus, fulfilling the "rumors" portion of verse 6 also. That too is why it appears to be Israel that verse 6 is referring to and not the nations <u>across the Earth</u>.

Additionally, for any who think Israel fulfilled verse 6 in the years immediately following the time of Jesus, don't. It is not possible that Jesus was referring to "wars and rumors of wars" relating to Israel back in His day, which was the very early 30s A.D. This is because they were under the Roman yoke and had no ability to engage in wars. Eventually they would rebel against Caesar and in 70 A.D. their scattering across the nations would begin unfolding. So it is not possible that this sequence discussed by Jesus in Matthew 24 verses 6-8 took place back in His day. Therefore, we are left with the restored Israel that is currently in the land to apply it to.

Also, we further know from the graphs located in this book's chapter titled, "Wars and Rumors of Wars," that wars <u>across the Earth</u> have, from a historical perspective, almost disappeared. Yes, there is fighting here and there seen on TV and with much banter made about it all. But, historically speaking, it is nothing compared to what has been before it. Beginning in the decade of the 1950s, the reduction of both wars and casualties from wars <u>across the Earth</u> have become the topic of scholarly debate because they are so notable a historical anomaly. There is, in a sense, a strange lull in such wars, which perfectly places the nations <u>across the Earth</u> in a position to rise when verse 7 begins unfolding. Far from that state of relative peace being in conflict with verse 6, the perspective presented here places it in perfect harmony once one realizes that verse 6, "wars and rumors of wars," applies to Israel and not the nations <u>across the Earth</u>. It is exactly what should be taking place as Israel is in her "rumors" phase.

By accepting that verse 6 relates to the condition of Israel, it is easy to identify which nation is involved in the "rumors of wars" with them. And that is, of course, Iran, with Hezbollah and Hamas thrown in the mix with the Iranians when the time comes. Simple logic tells us that verse 6 will not go on forever so, therefore, we know it will come to an end. This is because it must eventually come to an end so verse 7 can begin, because it is in a prophetic time frame that is prior to the beginning of verse 7. Therefore, it would appear that at some point in time Israel and Iran will complete verse 6 by either making peace and, thus, finally ending the "rumors" phase, or, more likely, finally go to war. Considering the nature of the Iranian regime, it is a challenge to imagine the "rumors" verse ending with a peace treaty between it and Israel. Therefore, for events to begin moving forward from verse 6, it would appear that Israel and Iran must go to war in order to fulfill the "rumors" verse. Such a war would probably be an ugly regional one. And a regional war in the Middle East is a very bad omen for the world.

A quick recap tells us that after the Israel-Iran war takes place, it is clear within Matthew 24:7 that at some point later in time another much bigger war will break out as "nation shall rise against nation" occurs. We also know that that war is the beginning of the birth pains because the Scripture tell us it is. By accepting that verse 6 and 7 are in different prophetic time frames, just prior to birth pains (verse 6), and then the beginning of birth pains (verse 7), a war between Israel and Iran in verse 6 must be over before the next war begins in verse 7. Consider the Matthew 24:6-8 one more time.

> ⁶ And ye shall hear of wars and rumours of wars: see that ye be not troubled: for all these things must come to pass, **but the end is not yet. (PRE BIRTH PAINS)**

> ⁷ For nation shall rise against nation, and kingdom against kingdom: and there shall be famines, and pestilences, and earthquakes, in divers places.

> ⁸ All these are **the beginning of sorrows. (BIRTH PAINS)**

So it is clear from these verses that the events in verse 6 must end before verse 7 begins, and they cannot be blended together because they are in different prophetic time frames. Some might consider that once war between Israel and Iran breaks out in completion of the "rumors" in verse 6, that "nation shall rise against nation" from that war immediately. But that cannot be. The reason why is if the two events somehow blended together, it would contradict the fact that both are clearly stated as happening within two different prophetic time frames. Also, additional Scripture that is connected to Matthew 24:7-8 appears to clearly indicate that there will first be another notable event, which will occur after the Israel-Iran war, dividing it from the "nation shall rise against nation" war even further.

A Shocking Attack

In Matthew 24:7-8, we find a critical link that connects it to another Scripture that fills in more details of what will unfold prior to the war between the nations across the Earth, and also what event will trigger it. This link exists because we are told the war between the nations in Matthew 24:7-8 will mark the "beginning of sorrows," or birth pains. Remember, the Scripture is not leaving it to our imagination as to what that war will represent; it is telling us it is the birth pains because of the qualifier in verse 8 that, "All these are the beginning of sorrows." But knowing that this war between nations is the start of birth pains also allows us to interlock this Scripture with another Scripture that identifies birth pains as well, with the specific detail of how they begin and what will come before them. So it allows us to be able to fill in another sequence of events that will unfold after the Israel-Iran war, but before that war between nations. Now consider Matthew 24:7-8 again but this time in conjunction with 1 Thessalonians 5:1-3 and how the description in both represent the prophetic moment of birth pains and also conflict.

Matthew 24:7-8

[7] For **nation shall rise against nation**, and kingdom against kingdom: and there shall be famines, and pestilences, and earthquakes, in divers places. (**CONFLICT**)

[8] All these are the beginning of sorrows. (**BIRTH PAINS**)

I Thessalonians 5:1-3

[1] But of the times and the seasons, brethren, ye have no need that I write unto you.

[2] For yourselves know perfectly that the day of the Lord so cometh as a thief in the night.

[3] For when they shall say, Peace and safety; **then sudden destruction cometh** upon them, (**CONFLICT**)

as travail upon a woman with child; and they shall not escape. (**BIRTH PAINS**)

Both Scriptures refer to certain events of conflict that happen and represent prophetic **birth pains**. In the Book of Matthew we are told it is "the beginning of sorrows," and in Thessalonians it is "as travail upon a woman with child." Both are referring to **birth pains**. So by being able to connect 1 Thessalonians 5:1-3 to Matthew 24:7-8, we are able to fill in a number of events that take place after an Israel-Iran war located in Matthew 24:6, but which happen before the outbreak of the war where "nation shall rise against nation" in Matthew 24:7. Additionally, we see how the war between the nations begins. Lets first look at how the war where "nation shall rise against nation" appears to begin.

I Thessalonians 5:2-3

> ² For yourselves know perfectly that the day of the Lord so **cometh as a thief in the night.** (IT IS UNEXPECTED)

> ³ For when they shall say, Peace and safety; **then sudden destruction cometh upon them,** (IT IS SUDDEN DE-STRUCTION)

The war between the nations comes "as a thief in the night," and with "sudden destruction." This tells us how that war mentioned in Matthew 24:7 begins because both events are connected by these birth pains. The beginning of the war where "nation shall rise against nation" will be a shock comparable to finding a thief in your home in the middle of the night. It will involve a very sudden and unexpected attack. And this attack will shock the nations it is perpetrated against. The Scripture is, again, not leaving it to us to imagine the context in which the conflict will begin because it is telling us it will be by "sudden destruction." It will not be from a dispute that grows and grows until the parties begin exchanging blows. It will be like Pearl Harbor, or September 11, 2001, in which it arrives out of the blue. And it will, no doubt, be a great shock to the world. But although it will be a great shock and surprise to the world, it will not be a surprise to some. Look at the next three verses that follow and in the context of the suddenness and the surprising nature of the attack that starts the war of Matthew 24:7. It is clear that some will not be surprised.

I Thessalonians 5:4-6

> ⁴ **But ye, brethren, are not in darkness, that that day should overtake you as a thief.** (THOSE WITH UNDERSTAND-ING WILL NOT BE SURPRISED)

⁵ Ye are all the **children of light**, and the children of the day: we are not of the night, nor of darkness. (THE CHILDREN OF LIGHT WILL NOT BE SURPRISED)

⁶ **Therefore let us not sleep, as do others; but let us watch and be sober.** (THERE IS SOMETHING TO WATCH FOR THAT WILL ALERT THOSE SOBER AND WATCHFUL THAT THE SHOCKING ATTACK IS AP-PROACHING)

Although in verses 2 and 3 it is clear that a war begins with "sudden destruction" that comes like "a thief in the night," it will not be a surprise to those "not in darkness." And the "children of light" who are not surprised are those who do "not sleep, as others do." As a result of not sleeping to the signs of its approach, they will "watch and be sober" during that time. Since the believer is exhorted to "watch and be sober," that means that there is something to watch for. That means that it is not only possible, but we are assured that those who do "not sleep" and "watch and be sober" will see it coming. Obviously, since it will be a great shock to the world, they will not see its terrible approach. Since it is typical of the world to ignore biblical warnings, this is why only the "children of light" who are "sober" will be able to see it. This is because the Bible is telling the "children of light" what to look for.

In addition to the sequence of Scripture described herein which lead the "sober" "children of light" to be able to discern its approach, there is a series of events occurring since 1991 that appears to represent something else worthy of consideration that appears to be a prophetic warning which confirms what is written here. It is the peculiar series of "coincidences" that has been repeating the same warning like a broken record. Consider the thirteen "coincidences" discussed in *The Israel Omen* and *The Israel Omen II*.

Within both books thirteen unique "coincidences" since 1991 are looked at. They involve efforts to remove the biblical Promised Land from Israel coinciding with historically significant disasters most often to the day the diplomatic effort began. They are a very strange litany of events that from a secular perspective are impossible to happen, and must be relegated to that of "coincidences." But from a biblical perspective these "coincidences" are not surprising. It is possible to attribute all of them to a fantastic chain of the most improbable coincidences, but it is not possible to deny that these "coincidences" have been happening. This is because there is no denying the correlation of the dates of the historically significant disasters' juxtaposition to the dates of the diplomatic efforts that have taken place. And here are a couple of observations concerning this series of "coincidences." They all have involved only historically significant disasters, no run-of-the-mill common type of calamities here. For anyone attempting to match up such disasters with another geopolitical event, this fact dramatically reduces the available ones to look at. Good luck trying because it has not been done yet. Also, remember, we are now talking about thirteen since 1991! And the other observation is that these "coincidences" appear to only occur during a move against the Promised Land that is a form of advance against it, not just a meeting that was completely insignificant with no "progress." Here is a brief example of just three of them, but all thirteen since 1991 until 2011 meet these criteria.

Hurricane Andrew

The "Madrid Peace Process held its sixth gathering in Washington D.C. on August 24, 1992, and it was the first one where real progress was made. Present for the first time was the new Israeli Prime Minister, Yitzhak Rabin. What made Rabin's presence so important was that he strongly favored trading the Promised Land for a peace treaty with the Palestinians and their Arab allies. As a result at that particular conference, great "progress" would be made which would soon result in the transferring of Israeli control over a portion of the Promised Land to the Palestinians. On that same day Hurricane Andrew went ashore in South Florida as the worst hurricane in U.S. history in terms of the cost of damage.[1]

September 11, 2001

In August of 2001, the leaders of Saudi Arabia were enraged with the Bush Administration's handling of the Israeli-Palestinian issue, accusing them of being too one-sided. In an effort to placate them, the Bush Administration decided on a historical shift in U.S. policy relating to the conflict. For the first time the United States would announce that it supported the establishment of a Palestinian state in the middle of the Promised Land. Essentially, this new policy would seek to permanently remove these lands biblically promised to the restored Israel. The date for the big rollout of the new policy, with much fanfare, was the week of September 10, 2001.[2]

Katrina

In the name of "peace" the Bush Administration sought the removal of Gaza from the Israelis, transferring it to the control of the Palestinians. Eventually, the president was able to convince the Israeli Prime Minister at the time, Ariel Sharon, that it was a good idea. In line with that, the Israeli government began an unpleasant process of removing their citizens from Gaza. The Israeli government declared their removal officially completed on August 23, 2005. On August 23, 2005, the same day that the removal of the land was completed, removing Jews from a portion of the Promised Land, a tropical depression that would become Katrina was first noticed by the National Hurricane Center. And it would soon begin removing many from their homes (including this author).[3]

THE COMING MIDEAST WAR AND PEACE TREATY

Why was it important for us to look at this phenomenon while our focus was on the Scriptures in Matthew 24:7-8 and 1 Thessalonians 5:2-3? It is because all thirteen "coincidences" of disasters striking with timing eerily associated with efforts to remove the Promised Land have three common denominators associated with them. All were done in the name of "peace," all experienced "destruction," and it was "sudden," coming usually on the day the effort to remove the land was started. See if these three common denominators sound familiar. They are "peace ... then sudden destruction," the same as the warning in 1 Thessalonians 5:2-3. And this reframe has been playing since 1991 at least thirteen times like a broken record and representing something that, perhaps, God's "children of light" should "watch and be sober" of. But it also carries with it a natural logical conclusion.

Since the thirteen "coincidences" have all involved historically significant disasters, it infers that the culmination of those warnings will have to be a magnitude significantly greater. That is because warnings must not be greater than that they warn of. That is simple logic. It is like the warnings to a child that a spanking is drawing near. The warnings are unpleasant, but not nearly so as the event. And all of those efforts since 1991 aimed toward "peace" succeeded in only making small moves against the land which will be dwarfed by a peace treaty between Israel and the Palestinians that establishes a new state called Palestine. Considering that all thirteen events were historically significant disasters associated with those small advances, then what will happen at the conclusion of those warnings where an actual peace treaty "permanently" removes the land? Such a conclusion of those warnings since 1991 should be on a scale vastly worse, and like the previous thirteen should be ushered in by sudden destruction as well. It all too perfectly fits the warning in 1 Thessalonians 5. Therefore, the only thing that brings a completion of all this is a peace treaty that finally removes the land from Israel for a Palestinian state.

Israel and a Treaty with Many

By connecting Matthew 24:7 to 1 Thessalonians 5:2-3 we are also able to see that a peace treaty between Israel and the Palestinians will happen before the war where "nation shall rise against nation." This is because the world will be declaring "peace and safety" before the "sudden destruction" that ushers in that war takes place. Consider the Scripture.

> ³ For **when they shall say, Peace and safety**; then sudden destruction cometh upon them, (IT'S A PEACE TREATY!)

And the Scripture is very clear that it is only after this peace treaty that the birth pains begin with sudden destruction, which ushers in the war where "nation shall rise against nation." And the peace treaty will be between Israel and the Palestinians, and not between Israel and the Iranians. One reason why this will be the case is the notable hatred for Israel within the Iranian leadership, making it difficult to imagine that after an Israel-Iran war those two will sign a peace treaty. It will likely be a war that will only end when shots stop being fired. To think the Iranians, who have voiced a desire time and again to eliminate Israel as a people, will then agree to a peace treaty with them after having had their nuclear facilities bombed is highly unlikely. And a little further along we will see that additional Scripture gives us a strong reason to believe that the peace treaty will be between Israel and the Palestinians. Instead, with the unfolding international situation against Israel, especially at the United Nations and also within the Obama Administration, the war between Israel and Iran will be the final straw before the world imposes a peace settlement on the only dispute in the troubled region that they can. And that dispute is the one between Israel and the Palestinians. Considering that President Obama has already aligned his peace plan closely to that of both the United Nations as well as what the Palestinians want, it is all lined up to unfold when the time comes. All Obama has to do now is to withdraw his veto the next

time the U.N. seeks to establish a Palestinian state. Now, let's look again at
1 Thessalonians 5:2-3.

I Thessalonians 5:2-3

> [2] For yourselves know perfectly that the day of the Lord so **cometh as a thief in the night.** (IT IS VERY SUDDEN)
>
> [3] For **when they shall say, Peace and safety**; then sudden destruction cometh upon them, (IT ALL HAPPENS AS THE WORLD IS SAYING IT'S PEACE!)

We know it is the world that will be saying peace due to the peace treaty, but not the "children of light" because they know better, at least those that are "sober." So what we are seeing here is that after an Israel-Iran war, but before the war where, "nation shall rise against nation," there will be a significant peace treaty that will be consummated. Allowing those with understanding to know that the next prophetic event on the horizon is a great war between the nations and that it will come suddenly. Adding to the case that this treaty will be between Israel and the Palestinians are the thirteen reframes since 1991 of peace and sudden destruction. Can that really just be another coincidence? And they all related to efforts to remove the lands from Israel in the name of peace with the Palestinians. And we know that any peace treaty settling the dispute will involve the removal of Judah (West Bank) and East Jerusalem.

Also, consider this. Almost all major efforts to resolve the Israeli-Palestinian dispute have involved a number of nations. There is the Quartet's effort consisting of the United States, Russia, European Union, and United Nations, which has held a number of conferences wherein a multitude of nations attended. And, also, there is the effort in the United Nations to establish a Palestinian state. Both have involved a number of nations in the mix. In fact, it is quite likely that any peace treaty between the Israelis and Palestinians will involve a multitude of nations, as a form of reassurance to the Israelis. And a little further along we will look at another Scripture that also connects with these events that states it will be "all nations" that "parted my land." That is an interesting term because all nations is exactly what the United Nations is. Therefore, if "all nations" are involved in parting the land in the name of peace, then where should the prophetic fallout go once the lands are finally removed? Would it not be the "nations" that eventually rise against one another, suffering a terrible war and its horrific consequences just as is indicated in Matthew 24:7?

Here is something else to consider. Of the thirteen "coincidences" where advances against the Promised Land lined up with historical disasters, one of them is an anomaly that stands out. In twelve of the "coincidences" advances made against the Promised Land coincided with a historical disaster that was NOT in the form of an attack. However, one did coincide with a sudden and dastardly attack and that was, of course, on September 11, 2001. What is notable here is that the diplomatic move against the land in that single case involved a shift of U.S. policy to support the establishment of a Palestinian state for the first time. Never before had a U.S. Administration made it official policy to support the creation of a Palestinian state. In other words, in line with that move toward a Palestinian state, which the 2001 policy shift represented, a sudden attack was experienced. Now consider where we are in the sequence of events so far. We have determined that a peace treaty that will "permanently" remove large tracts of land from Israel for the creation of a Palestinian state will happen. Then the Scripture tells us that a sudden attack will take place. The attack is so serious that "nation shall rise against nation." It would appear that the terrible September 11, 2001 attack was an omen of the "sudden destruction" promised "when they say peace." And none of the other twelve "coincidences" involved an attack.

THE COMING MIDEAST WAR AND PEACE TREATY

Signs in the Heavens

Now that we have connected 1 Thessalonians 5:1-3 to the war where "nation shall rise against nation," there is a phrase within those verses that allows us to make another connection to more Scripture relating to these events. In this case we are led to certain signs that will appear in the heavens. Let's look at 1 Thessalonians 5:1-3 again but with our focus on a different phrase within it.

I Thessalonians 5:1-3

¹ But **of the times and the seasons**, brethren, ye have no need that I write unto you.

² For yourselves know perfectly that **the day of the Lord** so cometh as a thief in the night. (A TIME AND SEASON)

³ For when they shall say, Peace and safety; then sudden destruction cometh upon them, as **travail upon a woman with child**; and they shall not escape. (BIRTH PAINS)

The Scripture is telling us that the unfolding events are a sign of the "times and the seasons." And then it gets even more specific stating that these birth pains, which are ushered in by the "sudden destruction," mark the beginning of where "nation shall rise against nation" (MT 24:7) and are the beginning of "the day of the Lord." So these verses are associating "the day of the Lord" with the beginning of birth pains or, as it states, "as travail upon a woman with child." Again, it is clearly stated in these verses that this "sudden destruction" marks "the day of the Lord" and birth pains. This *particular* "day of the Lord" appears to begin at the exact start of the prophetic birth pains. But regardless of the various concepts regarding "the day of the Lord," this Scripture associates the birth pains starting with "sudden destruction" with "the day of the Lord." It will "come as a thief in the night," after a peace treaty and arrives with "sudden destruction." So now that we can associate all of this with "the day of the Lord" in 1 Thessalonians 5, let's look at another Scripture that uses "the day of the Lord" as a reference for its unfolding prophetic events also: Joel 2:31.

Joel 2:31

> ³¹ The **sun shall be turned into darkness, and the moon into blood**, before the great and terrible **day of the LORD** come. (SOLAR ECLIPSE AND BLOOD MOONS BEFORE THE DAY OF THE LORD)

In Joel 2:31 "the day of the Lord" is referenced and it is in connection with an unusual astronomical event: the "sun shall be turned into darkness, and the moon into blood." From the chapter in this book titled, "Signs in the Heavens," we know about the significance of blood moons. And we know that when they fall on the Jewish feast days of Passover and the Feast of Tabernacles, in successive years, they are a rare and significant event that is referred to as a "tetrad." We also know about their history since 32-33 A.D., and we know that when records relating to the Jews are clear and available we can connect those tetrads to significant events associated with them. And today it is Israel that represents the Jews. So this passage would appear to be indicating that prior to **"the day of the Lord,"** there will be notable blood moons taking place. The verse also indicates that the sun will be turned into darkness during the time of these blood moons, which appears to be referring to a solar eclipse. Since we have a connection to **"the day of the Lord"** in this Scripture, just as we do in 1 Thessalonians 5, let's look at verses 30 and 31 together.

THE COMING MIDEAST WAR AND PEACE TREATY

Joel 2:30-31

> [30] And I will shew **wonders in the heavens** and in the earth, **blood, and fire, and pillars of smoke**. (WONDERS IN THE HEAVENS AND WAR ON THE EARTH)
>
> [31] The **sun shall be turned into darkness, and the moon into blood**, before the great and terrible **day of the LORD** come. (SOLAR ECLIPSE AND BLOOD MOONS BEFORE THE DAY OF THE LORD)

Now we see that in verse 30 that there will be some kind of "wonders in the heavens," and a war on the Earth noted by "blood, and fire, and pillars of smoke," as well as blood moons and a solar eclipse, with all of it beginning before the "day of the Lord" starts. So it would appear that the war mentioned in verse 30 is referring to the Israel-Iran war expected in this presentation, since it comes before "the day of the Lord." Put another way, this Scripture appears to be telling us that the war warned of in Matthew 24:7 where, "nation shall rise against nation," will come sometime after a blood moon and a solar eclipse appear. Now consider the entire sequence of events here.

There will be wonders in the heavens

There will be a war.

Blood moons and solar eclipses.

"The day of the Lord."

This sequence fits within the one established by Matthew and 1 Thessalonians which is a war between Israel and Iran (blood, and fire, and pillars of smoke), later followed by a great war (day of the LORD where "nation shall rise against nation.") However, this broad overview includes new information of what to look for within that sequence of events: heavenly wonders found in Joel 2:30-31. So before the blood moons and the solar eclipse we are told to look for, there will be these "wonders in the heavens." Now consider the year 2013 as it relates to heavenly wonders.

It begins with an asteroid that came closer to Earth than any of similar size ever has since NASA began gazing upward and took place on February 15.[4] Then two days later an asteroid streaked through the sky of Russia, the likes of which has not happened in over 100 years, startling the world and exploding with the power of a nuclear bomb 18 miles high.[5] Coming later in 2013 is Comet ISON, which experts say will be visible to the naked eye sometime in October and November. Now consider the *Universe Today* headline concerning 2013, "The Year of the Comets: Three Reasons Why 2013 Could be the Best Ever."[6] Indeed, expected in 2013 are three comets that should be visible to the naked eye. Consider this quote from another article on the approach Comet ISON.

> Since it is very well placed for viewing from the northern hemisphere during the weeks afterward, it could become one of the best and brightest comets of the past several centuries.[7]

The online magazine *Space.com* noted that ISON will likely join the nine most brilliant comets ever seen.[8] A Fox News headline proclaimed "2013 Comet May be Brightest Ever Seem."[9] The anchor for NBC Nightly News, Brian Williams, proclaimed ISON "A comet to watch in 2013" and that it could stretch across the day time sky 15 times brighter then the full moon.[10] So this raises the following question. Is all of this unusual activity in the heavens nothing more than a coincidence, occurring just before the coming tetrad of 2014-15? Now let's continue to look at the verses in the Book of Joel. The last verse in Joel 2, which is verse 32, urges people to turn to God in that difficult time. But the prophetic passages pick up again in the next two verses, Joel 3:1-2.

Joel 3:1-2

[1] For, behold, **in those days, and in that time,** when I shall bring again the captivity of Judah and Jerusalem,

> ² I will also gather **all nations**, and will bring them down into the valley of Jehoshaphat, and will plead with them there for my people and for my heritage Israel, whom they have scattered among the nations, **and parted my land.**

Joel 3:1 provides an understanding of the general time when the heavenly signs will take place prior to "the day of the Lord." And it is in the time when the Jews are brought back to the land of Israel. (THE TRANSLITERATION OF "BRING AGAIN THE CAPTIVITY OF JUDAH AND JERUSALEM" READS "WHEN I TURN BACK THE CAPTIVITY OF JUDAH AND JERUSALEM,") Then in that time when they are brought back, a significant event occurs wherein those against Israel will part the land. Notice that the land was not won in a war by an aggressor, but was parted as noted in verse 2 by the phrase "and parted my land." And the most likely way of parting land without a war is a negotiated settlement, or, peace treaty. And who parted it? That answer is also given in verse 2 as "all nations" indicated in the first line of the verse. The Lord is explaining why He has a problem with them, and it is for having "parted my land." Such a parting of the lands in dispute between Israel and the Palestinians is exactly what "all nations" have been attempting to do through the United Nations, and this further confirms that the expected treaty will be between Israel and the Palestinians, not Israel and the Iranians. This also adds more fuel to the notion of a peace treaty removing the lands from Israel. Additionally, at no other time in world history could "all nations" be involved in parting the land from Israel. It is only now with the United Nations that this is possible. Also, since we have seen the "coincidences" of disasters befalling those attempting to scatter the Promised Land, now this Scripture is telling us that the "nations" will part it. Now consider this.

Since it is the "nations" that will be involved in parting the land as a part of a peace treaty, then where is it reasonable to think the repercussions of that action will fall? It should justly befall those nations. Consider again the sequence of events that the Scriptures appear to be revealing. We are looking for "wonders in the heavens," and an Israel-Iran war, then sometime after that war, a peace treaty between the Israelis and Palestinians, parting the land and done by all nations through the U.N. We see the approach of a solar eclipse and blood moons coming in 2014-2015. Sometime within the "peace" process, a war between the nations is ushered in by sudden destruction representing the beginning of birth pains and "the day of the Lord." It is also significant that it is telling us this peace treaty will involve many nations and, thus, be a treaty between Israel and many. Or put another way, it will initiate a covenant with many and Israel. Since we know that the United Nations is now well-positioned by President Obama to accomplish the dark deed, we also know it is the essence today of many nations. Additionally, we know that the 2013 U.N. report concerning Palestinian statehood efforts are being guided by a plan drafted by the Quartet and referred to as the "roadmap." As mentioned in this book's chapter titled, "Supernatural Times," we see that a good case can be made that the Quartet is the "four horns" warned of by the old prophet Zechariah.11 There is great harmony between the Scriptures and geopolitical conditions.

Now let's look at another Scripture that provides a very broad overview of events that will unfold with the Jews and also includes heavenly signs.

Luke 21:24-25

> [24] And they shall fall by the edge of the sword, and shall be led away captive into all nations: and Jerusalem shall be trodden down of the Gentiles, until the times of the Gentiles be fulfilled.

[25] And there shall be **signs in the sun, and in the moon, and in the stars**; and upon the earth **distress of nations, with perplexity**; the sea and the waves roaring; (SIGNS GIVEN IN THE SUN, MOON AND STARS, AND A GREAT WAR BETWEEN THE NATIONS)

It is Jesus who is providing a very broad rendition of events that would unfold sometime in the future, which again, He was speaking sometime in the early 30s A.D. In verse 24, He warns of the coming Jewish Diaspora in which the Jews would be scattered across the nations of the world after falling to the sword of Rome. History tells us that this process began happening in 70 A.D. with Rome's legions finally breaking through Jerusalem's defenses and ultimately destroying the Holy Temple there. As such, Jerusalem was from that point forward "trodden down of the Gentiles" since the city was no longer possessed by the Jews. Then verse 24 takes us all the way to the completion of the Gentiles controlling Jerusalem with, "until the times of the Gentiles be fulfilled." We know historically that the "times of the Gentiles" were fulfilled in the Six-Day War in June of 1967 wherein the Jews captured East Jerusalem, which resulted in their possessing all of Jerusalem again for the first time since 70 A.D. So that one verse is a very broad view of Jewish history covering almost 1,900 years.

Since we know that a tetrad of blood moons occurred in the years 1967 and 1968, we can assume the heavenly sign was marking the great event of Jerusalem no longer being "trodden down of the Gentiles." So now let's focus on verse 25 concerning those heavenly signs.

Luke 21:25

[25] And there shall be **signs in the sun, and in the moon, and in the stars**; and upon the earth **distress of nations, with per-**

plexity; the sea and the waves roaring; (SIGNS GIVEN IN THE SUN, MOON AND STARS, AND A GREAT WAR BETWEEN THE NATIONS)

This verse is indicating that associated with "signs in the sun, and in the moon, and in the stars," there will be "distress of nations, with perplexity," which would appear to be the exact sequence of events related to us in Joel. Here are both Scriptures together.

Joel 2:31

31 The sun shall be turned into darkness, and the moon into blood, before the great and terrible day of the LORD come.

1. 1. SIGNS GIVEN BY THE SUN AND THE MOON AND
2. THE WAR BETWEEN NATIONS WITH SUDDEN DESTRUCTION MARKING ITS BEGINNING

Luke 21:25

25 And there shall be signs in the sun, and in the moon, and in the stars; and upon the earth distress of nations, with perplexity; the sea and the waves roaring;

1. SIGNS GIVEN BY THE SUN AND THE MOON AND
2. NOTABLE DISTRESS OF NATIONS MIXED WITH PERPLEXITY

The sequence appears to be the same if we see the distress of the nations as relating to a war. It is interesting that those nations are perplexed. That "perplexity" could be a result of "waves roaring," but it could also be from the shocking "sudden destruction" that happened. But whatever it is, this we know: there will be signs in the heavens associated with the nations of the Earth experiencing great troubles. And this is where all of that takes us.

We know that these tetrads are rare and have marked significant events for the Jews and Israel. Since the last tetrad occurred in 1967-68, it clearly applied to the events that unfolded at that time in which the Jews retook Jerusalem and ended the biblical time frame where the Gentiles had trodden down the city. So that biblical prophetic time frame ended in the year 1967 and was marked by the tetrad. In other words, the tetrad appeared to announce the end of a biblical prophetic time frame in that case. And we know that the next tetrad will take place in the years 2014-15. Again, think about it. We know from Luke 21:24 that the tetrad in 1967-68 marked the end of a significant prophetic time frame. Is it possible that the beginning of prophetic birth pains, another significant biblical prophetic time frame will be likewise announced? In fact, the Scriptures appear to tell us that it will be. Consider Joel 2:31, again focusing on the details provided in the heavenly signs.

Joel 2:31

> [31] The sun shall be turned into darkness, and the moon into blood, before the great and terrible **day of the LORD** come.

This sign in the heavens that comes before the day of the Lord, the war that suddenly breaks out among the nations representing prophetic birth pains will include not only blood moons, but a solar eclipse where the sun shall be turned into darkness. Now let's look briefly at the previous three tetrads. The one in 1493-94 involved the standard four blood moons falling in successive years on the Jewish feast days of Passover and the feast of Tabernacles. It coincided with the Jews' terrible expulsion from Spain, marking a monumental event in their history. The next tetrad happened in the years 1949-50 and coincided with the rebirth of the state of Israel. It consisted only of the four blood moons required for a tetrad. The last one occurred in 1967-68 and, again, involved only the required four blood moons on the above-mentioned Jewish feast days and coincided with the uniting of Jerusalem under Jewish control for the first time in almost 2,000 years. Now consider the next one set to arrive in 2014-15.

The coming tetrad for 2014-15 will, of course, have the required four blood moons occurring on Passover and the Feast of Tabernacles in those successive years. But unlike the others briefly reviewed here, it will also experience two solar eclipses within it as well. One solar eclipse will happen on March 20, 2015, the Jewish New Year, and the other on September 13, 2015, the Feast of Trumpets.[12] How rare is this for a tetrad? None of the last three had a solar eclipse happen on a Jewish feast day within the tetrad time frame.[13] And it appears that none of the four before that did. So unlike the previous tetrads, this one will involve "The sun shall be turned into darkness," along with the standard for a tetrad of "the moon into blood."

So as Jesus is speaking to His disciples on the Mount of Olives, it is His exhortation to look for "wars and rumors of wars" that represents a prophetic key, one able to unlock an array of other prophetic Scriptures. In consideration of all that has been said here, it would appear that the current Scriptural, geopolitical, and astrological situation in mid-2013 is pregnant, and ready to enter the birthing process.

* * * * *

Having considered the above array of Scripture and their harmonious relationship, it all results from viewing Matthew 24:6 verse, "wars and rumors of wars," as applying to Israel, and not the <u>nations of the Earth</u>. It is also the conclusion that verse 6 takes place in a separate prophetic time frame from verse 7. Once those conclusions are reached, then an array of other prophetic Scriptures begins to fit together confirming and reconfirming one another. And the flow of Scripture and conclusions from them leads the reader, inevitably, to the conclusion that the "times and seasons," warned of approach. However, it is important to note that nowhere herein is there any date established for anything to occur, except for the astronomical events, and they were determined by God and identified by computer programs that announce their approach.

If the war between Israel and Iran does not take place as indicated, then the thesis herein must begin to be seriously questioned. Indeed, should there not be the required "peace treaty" between Israel and the Palestinians, then the thesis is absolutely wrong and should be discarded. But if the indicated sequence of events begins to unfold, then those so inclined should "watch and be sober." And the sequence of events indicated here is quite simple to look for.

There must be a war between Israel and Iran, and it probably will be a regional one, although it does not have to be. After such a war, there should be a noticeable increase of pressure on Israel to agree to peace terms with the Palestinians, and the United Nations with its multitude of nations should be involved. Regardless of how it comes about, a peace treaty between Israel and the Palestinians should happen, and there should be an array of nations involved making it into, truly, a treaty with Israel and many. Those many nations will probably sign on to such a treaty with a commitment toward the survival of the newly vulnerable Israel, a commitment they will later break.

At some point in time, the Israeli lands sacrificed to the false peace will be removed from their possession in the name of peace. Within this season of "peace" there will be a moment of "sudden destruction," marking the beginning of the worst of times. And the season of when "sudden destruction" happens should reasonably be considered to last from the consummation of the treaty, until the lands are officially removed. Assuming that this is all correct, then the question arises as to when during this time they "say, Peace and safety," that the "sudden destruction" most likely to begin? And here we have a single example to look back upon.

It was the moment where the removal of Gaza from Israel was completed that the tropical depression, Katrina, was first discovered. In other words, after the removal of the land was completed. From a geopolitical standpoint, that kind of timing is probably more reasonable in the case of a peace treaty between Israel and the Palestinians. Why upset the process of removing the lands with a surprise attack before it is completed? We do not know who it is that engages in the dastardly act of "sudden destruction" that leads to nation against nation, but it is highly unlikely to be the U.S. or Israel that initiates it. In the case of the United States, why suddenly strike another nation at a point in time "when they shall say, Peace and safety?" The notion that Israel initiates it is equally unlikely. Why start a war after agreeing to a peace treaty? If they are that displeased with the terms, then just do not agree to it, and be ready to fight. But then in such a scenario a war would not be the surprise we are assured it will be. And the Scripture says that the words "Peace and safety" shall be heard. That does not sound like Israel resisting. What is more likely is that the war between Israel and Iran will leave a residue of hatred in its wake that is off the charts.

Although there are no dates set here, one should be weary of the coming season of the blood moons tetrad. Although we are told no man can know the day, we are also told to look for the seasons. Consider these Scriptures.

Matthew 16:2-3

> [2] He answered and said unto them, When it is evening, ye say,
> It will be fair weather: for the sky is red.

³ And in the morning, It will be foul weather today: for the sky is red and lowering. O ye **hypocrites**, ye can discern the face of the sky; but can ye not discern the **signs of the times?**

It is Jesus here who is sharply critical of those in His day that, although well able to discern coming weather, were blind to the "signs of the times." And His displeasure reaches the point of referring to them as "hypocrites."

Matthew 24:

³² Now learn a parable of the fig tree; When his branch is yet tender, and putteth forth leaves, ye know that summer is nigh:

³³ So likewise ye, when ye shall see all these things, know that it is near, even at the doors.

³⁴ Verily I say unto you, This generation shall not pass, till all these things be fulfilled.

³⁵ Heaven and earth shall pass away, but my words shall not pass away.

³⁶ **But of that day and hour knoweth no man**, no, not the angels of heaven, but my Father only.

In verse 33, Jesus is making it clear that as certain events begin to unfold, that those watching should, "know that it is near, even at the doors." But He points out that although we can know the seasons, and should, that no man knows the "day and hour." And, of course, there are the verses in 1 Thessalonians we are so well acquainted with.

I Thessalonians 5:1-4

¹ But of the times and the seasons, brethren, ye have no need that I write unto you.

² For yourselves know perfectly that the day of the Lord so cometh as a thief in the night.

³ For when they shall say, Peace and safety; then sudden destruction cometh upon them, as travail upon a woman with child; and they shall not escape.

⁴ But ye, brethren, are not in darkness, that that day should overtake you as a thief.

As we covered earlier, it is clear that not only are the "children of light" able to discern the "times and seasons," but they should! So in line with the Lord's admonitions, this book is an effort to "discern the signs of the times."

NOTE: A SUMMATION OF THE ABOVE SEQUENCE IS LOCATED IN APPENDIX B IN THE BACK OF THE BOOK

CHAPTER ELEVEN

Vortex of Events

W hat does it all mean when a no-name state senator is thrust into the leadership of the world's only super power in just four years through a series of the most unlikely breaks going his way? And strangely, each of those breaks either removed stronger opponents whom he had little chance of beating, or disabled a strong opponent from running an effective campaign. Those breaks also involved a global financial meltdown, as well as storms that were highly detrimental to others, but both occurring with timing that was greatly beneficial to him. Perhaps it means nothing, if there is no peculiar thrust to his presidency. But that is where his uncanny rise to power appears to intersect with his strange foreign policy. First, his presidency does, in fact, have a peculiar, even strident thrust relating to something: the Middle East. In fact, that thrust has altered the viability of Israel to its core by replacing a friendly dictator in Egypt that kept 40 years of peace with the Jews, with one steadfastly dedicated to the complete destruction of Israel: the Muslim Brotherhood. It is important to note this could not have happened without Barack Obama because he withdrew support from the friendly Hosni Mubarak, the long-time dictator of Egypt. It was Obama who signaled early in his administration a form of support for the outlawed group within Egypt. And with their rise to power they have replaced the peaceful Mubarak dictatorship with one dedicated to jihad. They are also dedicated to a revived Islamist caliphate. But it is not only Egypt where his actions produced sharp pains for Israel and the West.

His friendly policy toward the Muslim Brotherhood has undermined the nation of Jordan, also at peace with Israel, now threatened by a branch of jihadists associated with the Brotherhood. And it is clear that the ranks of the Syrian rebels, fighting against the terrible Assad, are dominated by, you guessed it, jihadists. If they win their battle to topple that dictator their new government will soon begin aiming for the destruction of Israel. Obama supports them as well. This dramatic shift within these three nations, all on Israel's borders, effectively would reconstitute the old alliance against her, the one that sought to "drive her into the sea" many years ago. And all of it rests squarely at the doorstep of President Obama. Without him in the White House, none of this would be unfolding. It was his administration from its inception that encouraged the Muslim Brotherhood, something no other president would have imagined doing. It was that action that ultimately spawned the entire dark litany mentioned. But there is more.

It is not in the interest of the United States or the West to see a Muslim caliphate revived in the Middle East. Yet, from the perspective of enabling such a reemerging empire, the president's actions have been everything the nation of Turkey could have hoped for. Should Turkey successfully exploit the "Arab Spring" and one day bring back under its wings the nations of its old caliphate, the one that World War I broke apart, then it will be Barack Obama's presidency that will mark the turning point that enabled it. And this is exactly what Islamists within the nation of Turkey have wanted. Those same Islamists were finally able to topple the only safeguard preventing their ascendency to power, the military. And this started early in the presidency of Mr. Obama, and no other U.S. president since 1924. Why would the Turkish military suddenly step aside from their traditional role of protecting the secular democracy that had existed there since 1924? What changed suddenly? Was it the result of an indication from Mr. Obama that caused them to step aside? It is only by changing a recurring action that a different result is produced.

Previous to Mr. Obama, and since 1924, the Turkish military protected the Nation's secular democracy from being taken over by Islamists. Obviously, something changed and quite early in Mr. Obama's first term. And with such a shifting of Turkey from secular democracy to an Islamist government, it is an ill omen for the West. And it is noted that of all the leaders in the world, Mr. Obama is closest to the Turkish leader. Whereas previous presidents were closest to leaders who held the same values as most Americans did. So the closeness of Mr. Obama to the Islamist Recip Erdogan of Turkey speaks volumes and supports the case that Mr. Obama has a strange view of what the Middle East should look like and raises the possibility that he is a supporter of pan-Arabism. If he is personally not affectionate to that concept, the impact of his policy in the region has still effectively promoted it.

The case that Mr. Obama has willfully spiked negotiations between the Israelis and Palestinians is solidly supported by his actions, of which even his strongest friends have been quite dismayed and critical. But here too we see a peculiar thrust to his actions. This is because by doing so it has driven the issue of conflict between the parties to the United Nations, where Israel is hopefully outnumbered. It is the same United Nations that approved an upgrade in the Palestinian status to "non-member state" so lopsidedly that it is apparent that Israel has almost no friends in the world body. And by directing the "peace" process toward the United Nations, he has checkmated tiny, but spunky, Israel into a corner. And the only reason such a choreographed set of events could have transpired is to accomplish a single goal: a forced peace treaty between Israel and the Palestinians. Some may feel his actions were necessary to finally get a "solution" to the intractable problem. Nevertheless, there is still this. Regardless of any piece of paper proclaiming "peace," true peace starts in the hearts of men. So such a "peace" will only make Israel much more vulnerable to extinction, just as it emboldens its foes. And it is increasingly apparent that the stage is set empowering the biased United Nations to bring about what previous U.S. presidents could not. And the reason why is because those previous presidents were not willing to sacrifice Israel's security. And that brings us to *The Israel Omen* events.

Within both *The Israel Omen* and *The Israel Omen II*, the thirteen historically significant disasters coinciding with efforts to remove the fabled Promised Land from Israel appear to have three common denominators associated with them: peace, destruction, and suddenness. This recurring theme relating to these strange events spell out the biblical warning of "Peace ... then sudden destruction" found in 1 Thessalonians 5:3. And if they constitute a Divine warning to those who "watch and [are] sober," they will only be noticed by those watching. If such historically significant disasters represent a warning, then the culmination of them will have to be a magnitude greater. If that is the case then these warnings, combined with the Middle East foreign policy of Mr. Obama, appear to intersect and represent an ill omen raising the following question: Is he the one who will bring *The Israel Omen* warnings to their conclusion with a "peace" agreement between Israel and the Palestinians? If so, he has only until 2016 to do it.

Coincidental to all of this occurring on the Earth through the person of Mr. Obama, in the heavens a rare tetrad approaches causing those of understanding to question what grand event relating to the Jews it will mark. And along with the coming tetrad are some other unusual celestial happenings. It is noted in Joel 2:30-31 that certain unusual heavenly wonders will occur before the sun being "turned into darkness, and the moon into blood," which appears to refer to the coming tetrad that has solar eclipses on Jewish feast days. Consider the Scripture and then the events that have begun unfolding.

Joel 2:30-31

> [30] And I will shew **wonders in the heavens** and in the earth, blood, and fire, and pillars of smoke. (WONDERS IN THE HEAVENS AND WAR ON THE EARTH)

> [31] The sun shall be turned into darkness, and the moon into blood, before the great and terrible day of the LORD come.

Before a sequence of events noted in the passage get going, it is indicated that there will appear "wonders in the heavens." And, indeed, it appears that this may already have begun. There have been unusual asteroids passing the Earth, and one of them streaked through the sky of Russia, a spectacle that bedazzled the world. And later in 2013, a great comet is set to pull the eyes of the world to the heavens.

With notable wonders in the heavens taking place in the year before "The sun shall be turned into darkness, and the moon into blood," set to happen in 2014-15, it is exactly as the Scriptural flow of events indicate should be taking place. Perhaps it is all a coincidence. Only time will tell. And as time passes, it will also tell us if Israel addresses the Iranian threat with war. In the sequence of events considered herein in order for Matthew 24:6 to be completed, there must be war between Israel and Iran.

After waiting ten years, Israel finally issued a red line relating to Iran, and, in fact, the world. It was their Prime Minister, Netanyahu, who, standing before the unfriendly United Nations, held forth a poster board with a red line drawn on it. It was a stark challenge to the multitude of nations that refuse to take effective action to prevent the mullahs of Tehran from obtaining nuclear weapons. As such, we know that Israel has placed its word on the line for all to see. And to not back it up will now result in additional dangers to the tiny nation. So if Matthew 24:6 is relating to a war between Israel and Iran, then the "rumors" will finally come to an end. And those "rumors" have been going on for about a decade, making them unique. Although the twentieth and twenty-first centuries have brought with them an assortment of "rumors of wars," none appear to have been as persistent as those between Israel and Iran. In conjunction with those "rumors" is an Israeli nation that since its coming back into the ancient lands, just as was prophesized, has been in a new war on average ever 4.6 years. And that is amazing.

The sequence of events presented here can be summed up in the following litany to look for. In the beginning there should be notable "wonders in the heavens," which, as of this writing in early June 2013, something akin to that appears to have been taking place in the first half of the year. And astronomers tell us that later in the year "Could be the Best Ever" for comets. If that is all another coincidence, then it is quite an odd one to be taking place in the year before the tetrad begins. Then at some point there should be a war between Israel and Iran, and, no doubt, if it unfolds will likely be a messy regional one. Some time thereafter, there should be a peace treaty between Israel and the Palestinians. And if all of this unfolds, as the narrative herein presented describes, then the last in the sequence would be the war between the nations, and it will come suddenly and shockingly to the world. This is the sequence of events that must unfold, or the thesis presented here is wrong.

However, if they unfold in the flow indicated, then it should be obvious, even to the skeptic, that supernatural times have arrived. If so, then these other observations should as well be considered. In the Book of Daniel there is a passage that relates to a peace agreement. Consider his old prophetic words.

Daniel 9:27

> [27] And **he shall confirm the covenant with many for one week:** and in the midst of the week he shall cause the sacrifice and the oblation to cease, and for the overspreading of abominations he shall make it desolate, even until the consummation, and that determined shall be poured upon the desolate.

There are many Bible scholars who believe this Scripture is referring to a terrible world leader who will engage in the action of confirming a peace agreement with Israel. Some think this means he will create one, others that it is already in existence and he will confirm it. The transliteration of the phrase is, "strengthened a covenant." On that basis it would appear already in existence and he will simply strengthen it. If the sequence of events presented in this book unfolds as indicated, then the peace treaty between Israel and the Palestinians may be the one that will later be confirmed, or strengthened. And the passage tells us that this action will do so for a period of seven years. Interestingly, the passage describes the "covenant," or treaty, as having a certain characteristic: it will be with many. If that sounds familiar, it should. If the sequence described in this book unfolds, then the "peace" treaty involving Israel should involve the unique characteristic of involving many nations. If it is to later be confirmed, then the initial treaty does not have to be for seven years. In fact, if this is the case, then it can be for any number of years.

There is something else to consider. There is debate among sincere people of where this world leader's kingdom will be formed. Some say it will be a European one, others of a Middle Eastern origin. If it is of the

Middle East then it will likely spring forth from the nation of Turkey's efforts to reconstitute its caliphate. Considering the landscape of the region, it is difficult to see another nation able to pull it off. And with the soil for a new caliphate being well tilled during President Obama's time in office, all of this adds to the interesting nature of the current times.

APPENDIX A

The Thirteen Coincidences

October 30, 1991

- Madrid Middle East Peace Conference opens its doors. It is a breakthrough that gets the warring parties talking, with the ultimate goal the removal of large portions of the "Promised Land"

- The worst of the "Perfect Storm" strikes the bewildered England coast, described by weather experts as a "once in a 100 year freak of nature."*

August 24, 1992

- Round six of the Madrid Peace effort begins in Washington D.C. with a new Israeli leader, Rabin at the helm. For the first time the "land for peace" effort has a friend on the Israeli side and significant progress is made.

- Hurricane Andrew, the 4th most powerful storm ever to make landfall in the U.S. strikes. It devastates South Florida becoming the most expensive natural disaster in the nation's history.*

April 1993 until August 1993

- A historical peace agreement is negotiated over this time period, second only to the Camp David accord, it results in a removal of Israeli control over sections of the Promised Land"

- The "worst natural disaster in U.S. history" unfolds with several States inundated from continuous rains. Some say it was a 500 year flood, breaking records by the scores.*

January, 17 1994

- The day before President Clinton meets Syrian President Assad, they discuss the return of the Golan Heights from Israel. The following day Israeli Prime Minister Rabin warns the public to be prepared to return the Golan Heights.

- The highest ever recorded earthquake in an urban area strikes the U.S., causing the second most costly destruction caused by a natural disaster in U.S. history.*

June 5, 2001

- The new Bush Administration begins with a "hands off" approach to the Middle East conflict. Then the White House suddenly announces it is sending CIA Director George Tenet in an effort to implement proposals that would restrict Israeli use of the "Promised Land"

- A tropical storm suddenly appears off the Texas coast, after "It went right from nothing to a tropical storm!" It strikes the Houston area resulting in what would be called the "Great flood of 2001"*

September 10, 2001

- The week the Bush White House was ready for the "big rollout" of a major change in U.S. Middle East policy, becoming the first U.S. administration to support a Palestinian State on a large part of the "Promised Land."

- The next day, for the first time since Pearl Harbor, the U.S. is successfully attacked by a foreign enemy in a devastating assault.*

April 30, 2003

- The "long awaited" effort by the Quartet was kicked-off on this day. This new effort included the United States, Russia, European Union, and the United Nations. The goal is centered on removing large portions of the "Promised Land" for the creation of a Palestinian State.

- The "worst weather in U.S. history" begins on this day, ultimately resulting in 562 tornados over a span of about 4 weeks, accompanied by 1,587 hail storms and 740 reports of additional wind damage.*

June 2003 until August 2003

- Europe finally becomes an international player again and a major factor in the recent Quartet's effort to remove the "Promised Land" from Israel for the creation of a Palestinian State.

- The worst heat wave in over 250 years strikes Europe shortly after the "worst weather in U.S. history" ends. It devastates the continent with a terrible cost in lives.*

August 23, 2005

- The painful removal of Israeli citizens from large portions of the "Promised Land" is declared officially completed. Gaza is abandoned. About 5 months later Sharon is struck-down by a stroke. (NOTE: Old Jewish prophet Zaphaniah foretold a time would come when *"Gaza will be forsaken"*)

- Tropical depression number twelve is first noticed by the National Hurricane Center on this day. It is eventually named Katrina and soon becomes the most destructive natural disaster in U.S. history. Political advisors of President Bush, looking back in 2009, declare it was the beginning of the end of the Bush Presidency.*

Week of July 23, 2007

- Former British Prime Minister Tony Blair begins his first trip to the Middle East as Quartet envoy, ultimately leading to the Annapolis Conference where the world begins a renewed effort to pressure the Jews to give up large portions of the "Promised Land" for a Palestinian state. (NOTE: Old Jewish prophet Zachariah foretold a group of four powers will divide the "Promised Land" resulting in terrifying events against the nations.)

- The world financial system suffers a critical breakdown, bringing it to the brink of a systemic meltdown. It all begins this week when the bank-to-bank loan premium begins an event statistically estimated should happen 1 day out of every 2,500,000.

April 14, 2010

- The British advertising standards Authority votes for the removal of Israeli tourism posters showing East Jerusalem as a part of Israel. The implication is that it is not part of Israel.

- A volcano on Iceland blows its top for only the 4th time since the year 1612, spewing over 250 million cubic meters of ejected ash into the atmosphere. It shuts down British air travel and tourism.

April 20, 2010

- The Obama Administration succeeds in causing Israel, for the first time since 1967, to cease construction in East Jerusalem. This action effectively reduces Israeli control ver the Holy City fully restored during the 1967 Six-Day war.

- British Petroleum's Deepwater Horizon oil rig explodes in the Gulf of Mexico, only to become the worst environmental disaster in history. It would devastate the seafood industry across the Gulf Coast, devastating the tourist trade as well.

Week of April 4, 2011

- The Obama Administration decides on a U.S. policy concerning Israeli control of the fabled "Promised Land." It is draconian and would represent not only the removal of large tracts of land, but place the small nation in a vulnerable position versus their enemies.

- The worst tornado rampage in world history begins, involving more than 875 confirmed twisters in the month of April 2011, surpassing the previous record of 575. It would also mark the beginning of flooding comparable to the great 1927 flood.

APPENDIX B

Summation
"The Sequence of Prophetic Events"

The Coming Israel-Iran War

The discernment that Matthew 24:6 and 7 are talking about different wars and are in different prophetic time frames is the key to opening up an array of prophetic Scriptures, allowing them to come together in harmony with one another. Verse 6, which focuses on "wars and rumors of wars," represents "the end is not yet," indicating **pre-birth pains**, and verse 7, "nation shall rise against nation," is described as "the beginning of sorrows," indicating the **birth pains** have now begun.

Pertaining to verse 6, we see that since Israel's beginning in 1948, the Jewish nation has experienced a war approximately every 4.6 years. We have also seen that they are internationally unique in terms of the persistent rumor of a major regional war with Iran. This rumor has been going on since about 2003. Yet, as Israel has been experiencing "wars and rumors of wars" unlike any other nation, the nations <u>across the Earth</u> have reached a place of uncanny peace. From a historical perspective, this certainly does not qualify the nations for fulfilling verse 6 of "wars and rumors of wars" or, for that matter, verse 7 at present, where "nation shall rise against nation." And since verse 6 and 7 are clearly in two different prophetic time frames, they do not blend together. So because we see that verse 6, "wars and rumors of wars" relates to Israel, we know that at some point the rumor phase must come to an end. The only realistic way that can happen is if the "rumors" become a war. Therefore, we know now that there will be a regional war between Israel and Iran. The other thing we know is that sometime after that Israel-Iran war, the nations will go to war against each other.

A Shocking Attack

Since Matthew 24:7 represents prophetic **birth pains**, we are able to connect it to another Scripture that also talks about those **birth pains**, 1 Thessalonians 5:2-3. Therein we are told what will happen during that time.

1 Thessalonians 5:2-3

> [2] For yourselves know perfectly that the day of the Lord so cometh as a thief in the night.
>
> [3] For when they shall say, Peace and safety; then sudden destruction cometh upon them, **as travail upon a woman with child**; and they shall not escape.

Here too we see the prophetic **birth pains** again but, this time, they are associated with more details of what will happen that brings them on. We are told that they will begin by "sudden destruction." Since both

Matthew 24:7 and 1 Thessalonians 5:3 are involved in the start of birth pains, and then conflict, they have to be talking about the same event. Therefore, we know that the wars pitting nation against nation in Matthew 24:7 will begin with sudden destruction. In other words, it will not be a war that gradually develops. But we also are being told what will happen prior to the initiation of that "sudden destruction."

Israel and a Treaty with Many

Just prior to the "sudden destruction" that leads into the wars between the nations, something else we are told will happen. Notice the bold print in verse 3.

I Thessalonians 5:2-3

> [2] For yourselves know perfectly that the day of the Lord so **cometh as a thief in the night.**
>
> [3] For **when they shall say, peace and safety**; then sudden destruction cometh upon them, as travail upon a woman with child; and they shall not escape.

So now we know that just prior to the war between the nations ushered in by "sudden destruction," there will be a peace treaty that will be the cause of much peace rhetoric. We know this because it is telling us that words of "peace, and safety" will be heard.

But it is not just the flow of Scripture here that leads us to the belief that a moment of "sudden destruction" associated with a peace treaty will come about, it is also the litany of events covered in "coincidences" covered in *The Israel Omen* and *The Israel Omen II*.

These "coincidences" involve historically significant disasters occurring, often to the day, with advances against the Promised Land currently in Israel's possession and done in the name of peace. There are thirteen of them and they all have the same three common denominations: peace then sudden destruction. As such, it appears that since their beginnings in 1991 that a broken record type of warning has been playing to those who have observed this phenomenon. And it leads to the reasonable logic that if those previous small advances against the land in the name of peace brought about historically significant disasters, then the culmination of those warnings in a peace treaty that results in the "permanent" removal of those same lands should be a significant magnitude worse.

It is also clear that although the world will be greatly surprised by the sudden destruction that unfolds, causing nation to rise against nation, the "children of light" will not be. This is because they "are not in darkness," and so the events will not overtake them "as a thief." And the reason why is that they do not sleep, as others do, but are "sober."

But the whole terrible event will be a shock comparable to finding a thief in the middle of the night where they should not be. Then verses 4-6 clarify that there are some who will not be surprised.

I Thessalonians 5:4-6

[4] But ye, brethren, are not in darkness, that that day should overtake you as a thief.

[5] Ye are all the **children of light**, and the children of the day: we are not of the night, nor of darkness.

[6] Therefore let us not sleep, as others; but let us watch and be sober.

Essentially, the "children of God" who "watch and be sober" will not be surprised. And in line with that, they are urged to not sleep," but to stay awake and watch for the signs of the season.

Signs in the Heavens

Because we can connect 1 Thessalonians 5:1-3 with the unfolding events that bring on the season of prophetic **birth pains**, there is another Scripture in the Book of Joel that can now be connected. First, look again at 1 Thessalonians 5:1-3 but with the emphasis on another set of verses.

1 Thessalonians 5:2-3

> ¹ But of the **times and the seasons**, brethren, ye have no need that I write unto you.
>
> ² For yourselves know perfectly that **the day of the Lord** so cometh as a thief in the night.
>
> ³ For when they shall say, peace and safety; then sudden destruction cometh upon them, **as travail upon a woman with child**; and they shall not escape.

What we are seeing here are two important things. First, when the events described begin unfolding, the **"times and seasons"** warned of have begun. And what time and season would that be? The time of the **birth pains**. But it also provides another description of what this season represents, and that is **"the day of the Lord."** So the Scripture is directly connecting the birth pains with "the day of the Lord." Now that we are told that these **birth pains** mark the beginning of "the day of the Lord," we can connect them to another Scripture that also uses that phrase to describe certain events. And that takes us to the Book of Joel.

Joel 2:30-31 & Joel 3:1-2

> ³⁰ And I will shew **wonders in the heavens** and in the Earth, **blood, and fire, and pillars of smoke**.

³¹ The **sun shall be turned into darkness, and the moon into blood**, before the great and terrible **day of the LORD** come.

¹ For, behold, in those days, and in that time, when I shall bring again the captivity of Judah and Jerusalem,

² I will also gather all nations, and will bring them down into the valley of Jehoshaphat, and will plead with them there for my people and for my heritage Israel, whom they have scattered among the nations, and **parted my land**.

Connected to the "day of the Lord" are a series of Earthly and heavenly events that we are told will happen before it unfolds. It is telling us that before the "sudden destruction" where "nation shall rise against nation" begins, that these signs will take place. There will be "wonders in the heavens," and a war signified by "blood, and fire, and pillars of smoke." There will be other heavenly signs to come including the "sun shall be turned into darkness, and the moon into blood." Only then shall the "day of the Lord" begin. (nation shall rise against nation) Finally, the reason is given for its arrival and it is because the "nations" "parted my land." Now another Scripture from the Book of Luke that also talks about these same signs in the heavens.

Luke 21:24-25

²⁴ And they shall fall by the edge of the sword, and shall be led away captive into all nations: and Jerusalem shall be trodden down of the Gentiles, until **the times of the Gentiles be fulfilled.**

²⁵ And there shall be **signs in the sun, and in the moon, and in the stars**; and upon the earth **distress of nations, with perplexity**; the sea and the waves roaring;

We know the tetrad that took place in 1967-68 coincided with the moment that the "times of the Gentiles [were] fulfilled." We also see in this Scripture the same sequence of events that we observed in Joel 2:31 involving the sun and blood moons, followed by the distress of nations. But the unfolding tetrad for 2014-15 includes what the previous three did not, a solar eclipse on a Jewish feast day as well, which perfectly will fulfill the signs given prior to nation rising against nation. Which we also know represents the beginning of birth pains that mark another significant biblical prophetic time frame.

REFERENCES

Chapter One—When They Say Peace in the Mideast

1. *Holy Bible*, King James Version, Book of Genesis; Chapter 17
2. *Holy Bible*, King James Version, Book of Genesis; Chapter 19
3. www.Chabad.org, "The Contrast Between Isaac and Ishmael," http://www.Chabad.org/library/article_cdo/aid/1012030/jewish/The-Contrast-Between_Isaac-Ishmael
4. "Egypt-Israel Relations," Jewish Virtual Library, [accessed 06/10/2013] http://www.jewishvirtuallibrary.org/jsource/Peace/egtoc.html

Chapter Two—Supernatural Times

1. *Holy Bible*, King James Version, Book of John; Chapter 11
2. Ibid.
3. Ibid.
4. Ibid.
5. Ibid.
6. Gardiner, *The Admonitions of an Egyptian Sage*, (Georg Olms Verlag 1990)

7. Ibid.

8. *Holy Bible*, King James Version, Book of Zechariah; Chapter 12

9. Jonathan Cahn, *The Harbinger: The Ancient Mystery that Holds the Secret to America's Future* {Lake Mary, FL: Charisma House Book Group, 2012}

10. Ibid.

11. David Brennan, *The Israel Omen* {Metairie, LA: Teknon Publishing, 2009}

12. Ibid.

13. David Brennan, *The Israel Omen II* {Metairie, LA: Teknon Publishing, 2011}

14. Ibid.

15. David Brennan, *The Israel Omen* {Metairie, LA: Teknon Publishing, 2009}Ibid.

16. Ibid.

17. Ibid.

18. Ibid.

19. RedMoonRapture.com,

20. Philip Pullella, Reuters, "Pope's sudden resignation sends shockwaves through church," 2/11/13, http://www.reuters.com/article/2013/02/11/us-pope-resigns-idUSBRE91A0BH20130211

21. www.Space.com, "NASA Fireball Website Launches with New Russian Meteor Explosion Details," http://www.space.com/20216-russian-meteor-nasa-fireball-website.html

22. www.NationsEncyclopedia.com, "Vatican-Location, size, and extent,"

23. Jesse Farrell, www.Accuweather.com, "Did Lightning Really Strike Vatican After Pope's Resignation?"

Chapter Three—The Rise of Barack Obama

1. Kathy Gill, About.com, "Barack Obama," 1/3/2009 http://uspolitics.about.com/od/senators/a/barack_obama.htm?p=1

2. Drew Griffin and Kathleen Johnston, CNN.com, "Obama played hardball in first Chicago campaign," http://www.cnn.com/2008/POLITICS/05/29/obamas.first.campaign/

3. Jay Stone, "Obama's Strategy to Win at All Costs Violated His Challengers' Civil Rights," http://stoneformayor.com/obamas-strategy-to-win-at-all-costs-violated-his-challengers-civil-rights/

4. Ibid.

5. Ibid.

6. Fox News, "Ryan Drops Out of Ill. Senate Race," 06/25/2004, http://www.foxnews.com/story/0,2933,123716,00.html

7. Dennis W., *Free Republic*, "David Axelrod—Gets Obama's opponent's sealed divorce records opened up," 9/6/2008, http://www.freerepublic.com/focus/news/2075850/posts

8. Ibid.

9. Steve Kornacki, *New York Observer*, "A Brief History of Democratic Convention Keynotes," http://observer.com/2008/08/a-brief-history-of-democratic-convention-keynoters/

10. Ibid.

11. Nick Mathiason, *The Guardian*, "Three weeks that changed the world," http://www.guardian.co.uk/business/2008/dec/28/markets-credit-crunch-banking-2008

12. Ibid.

13. Ibid.

14. The Obama Files, http://theobamafile.com/_associates/obamaassociates.htm

15. Ibid.

16. Jim Rutenberg and Michael Shear, *The New York Times*, "As Storm Disrupts Plans, G.O.P. Takes Up Tensions," 08/27/2013, http://www.nytimes.com/2012/08/28/us/politics/romney-camp-looks-to-head-off-storm-during-convention.html?pagewanted=all&_r=0&pagewanted=print

17. Nate Silver, *The New York Times*, "Did Hurricane Sandy Blow Romney Off Course?" 11/5/2012 http://fivethirtyeight.blogs.nytimes.com/2012/11/05/nov-4-did-hurricane-sandy-blow-romney-off-course/

18. Grace Wyler, *Business Insiders*, "Insiders Explain How Mitt Romney's Campaign Completely Fell Apart On Election Day," 11/12/2012 http://www.businessinsider.com/romney-project-orca-election-day-collapse-2012-11

19. Ibid.

Chapter Four—Israel Surrounded

1. www.TheOttomans.org, History, http://www.theottomans.org/english/history/index.asp

2. www.HistoryLearningSite.com, "Palestine 1918 to 1948," http://www.historylearningsite.co.uk/palestine_1918_to_1948.htm

3. U.S. Department of State, Office of the Historian, ""Creation of Israel, 1948," http://history.state.gov/milestones/1945-1952/CreationIsrael

4. Jewish Virtual Library, "Israeli War of Independence Background & Overview," http://www.jewishvirtuallibrary.org/jsource/History/1948_War.html

5. *The New York Times*, "Egypt And Israel Sign Formal Treaty, Ending A State Of War After 30 Years; Sadat And Begin Praise Carter's Role," http://www.nytimes.com/learning/general/onthisday/big/0326.html

6. Caroline Glick, *Jerusalem Post* "Obama's Newest Ambush," May 17, 2011, http://www.jpost.com/Opinion/Columnists/Article.aspx?id=220307

7. Caroline Glick, *The Jerusalem Post*, "Obama's Abandonment of America," http://www.carolineglick.com/e/2011/05/obamas-abandonment-of-america.php

8. Caroline Glick, *The Jerusalem Post*, "Column One: The trap that Arik built," 11/22/2012 http://www.jpost.com/LandedPages/PrintArticle.aspx?id=293128

9. Ibid.

10. Encyclopedia Britannica, "Muslim Brotherhood," http://www.britannica.com/EBchecked/topic/399387/Muslim-Brotherhood

11. Newsmax, "Egypt Takes Dictatorial Powers," 11/22/2112, http://www.newsmax.com/Newsfront/Morsi-Egypt-dictatorial-powers/2012/11/22/id/465109?s=al

12. Oren Kessler, *The Jerusalem Post*, "Egypt Islamist vows global caliphate in Jerusalem," 08/05/2012, http://www.jpost.com/LandedPages/PrintArticle.aspx?id=269074

13. Imtiaz Gul, *The Express Tribune*, "Why not the Turkey way?" 03/14/2012 http://tribune.com.pk/story/349956/why-not-the-turkey-way/?print=true

14. Michael Rubin, National Review Online, "Erdogan's Agenda," 05/16/2013, http://www.nationalreview.com/node/348422/print

15. Ece Toksabay, Reuters, "Israelis on trial in Turkey over Gaza ship deaths," http://www.reuters.com/assets/print?aid=USBRE8A50Z420121106

16. Susan Fraser and Matthew Lee, Huff Post, "Recep Erdogan, Turkish Prime Minister, Zionism Remarks," http://www.huffingtonpost.com/2013/03/01/recep-erdogan-zionism_n_2788492.html

17. David Ignatius, *Washington Post*, "Obama's friend in Turkey," 06/07/2012, http://articles.washingtonpost.com/2012-06-07/opinions/35459692_1_obama-and-erdogan-obama-erdogan-turkish-leader

18. Mortimer Zuckerman, *The Wall street Journal*, "Obama's Jerusalem Stonewall: Demanding a Construction Freeze Reverses Decades of U.S. Policy," 04/27/2010, http://eyeonfreedom.com/index.php/obamas-jerusalem-stonewall-demanding-a-construction-freeze-reverses-decades-of-us-policy/

19. Charles Krauthammer, *The Washington Post*, "What Obama Did to Israel," May 25, 2011, http://www.washingtonpost.com/opinions/what-obama-did-to-israel/2011/05/26/AGJfYJCH_stry.html

20. Steven Myers, *The New York Times*, "Amid Impass in Peace Negotiations, America's Chief Middle East Envoy Resigns," May 13, 2011

21. Ibid.

22. Henry Reske & Kathleen Walter, Newsmax, Dershowitz: Obama Torpedoed Peace Process," May 20, 2011, Http://www.newsmax.com/printtemplate.aspx?nodeid+397146

23. Ben Hubbard, *The New York Times*, "Islamist Rebels Create Dilemma on Syrian Policy," http://www.nytimes.com/2013/04/28/world/middleeast/islamist-rebels-gains-in-syria-create-dilemma-for-us.html?pagewanted=all&_r=0

24. Mona Alami, *USA Today*, "Syrian rebels pledge loyalty to al-Qaeda," April 11, 2013, http://www.usatoday.com/story/

news/world/2013/04/11/syria-al-qaeda-connection/2075323

25. Sharona Schwartz, *The Blaze*, "Did You Know About the Surprising Views on Israel of Obama's Likely Pick for Secretary of Defense?" http://www.theblaze.com/stories/2012/12/17/did-you-know-about-the-surprising-views-on-israel-of-obamas-likely-pick-for-secretary-of-defense/

26. Ibid.

27. VOA News, Voice of America, "Panetta Tells VOA He Won't Step Down Right Away," November 15, 2012, http://www.voanews.com/articleprintview/1547127.html

28. Sharona Schwartz, *The Blaze*, "Did You Know About the Surprising Views on Israel of Obama's Likely Pick for Secretary of Defense?" http://www.theblaze.com/stories/2012/12/17/did-you-know-about-the-surprising-views-on-israel-of-obamas-likely-pick-for-secretary-of-defense/

29. Moshe Phillips, *American Thinker*, "John Kerry at State: A Disaster for Israel," http://www.americanthinker.com/2012/12/john_kerry_at_state_a_disaster_for_israel.html

30. Ryan Jones, *Israel Today*, "Kerry compares Israeli military to terrorists," http://www.israeltoday.co.il/NewsItem/tabid/178/nid/23805/Default.aspx

Chapter Five—Signs in the Heavens

1. *Holy Bible*, King James Version, Genesis; Chapter 1

2. *Holy Bible*, King James Version, Book of Luke; Chapter 2

3. Bob Abernethy, PBS, "Star of Bethlehem," http://www.pbs.org/wnet/religionandethics/?p=4677

4. *Holy Bible*, King James Version, Book of Matthew; Chapter 27

5. Eusebius' *Chronicle*, 202 Olympiad, (Phlegon's 13th book quote in Jerome's translation)

6.   Origen, *Against Caesar*

7.   Tertullian, *Apology*, No. 21 (Grand Rapids: Wm. B. Eerdmans Publishing Company, 1951), p. 35 in Vol. III of Anti-Nicene Fathers

8.   *Holy Bible*, King James Version, Book of Matthew; Chapter 27

9.   Eusebius' *Chronicle*, 202 Olympiad, (Phlegon's 13th book quote in Jerome's translation)

10. *Holy Bible*, King James Version, Book of Joel; Chapter 2

11. NASA, "Five Millennium Catalog of Lunar Eclipses," http://eclipse.gsfc.nasa.gov/LEcat5/LE0001-0100.html

12. http://Jewishholidaysonline.com/32 "Jewish Holidays for 32" ("33")

13. Shirat Devorah, "Blood Moon: Total Lunar Eclipse," http://shiratdevorah.blogspot.com/2011/06/blood-moon-total-lunar-eclipse.html

14. Blood Moon Rapture, http://www.redmoonrapture.com/crucifixion

15. Ibid.

16. Ibid.

17. Ibid.

18. Jewish Virtual Library, "The Spanish Expulsion 1492," http://www.jewishvirtuallibrary.org/jsource/Judism/expulsion.html

19. Ibid.

20. Ibid.

21. Ibid.

22. Jewish Virtual Library, "The Diaspora," http://www.jewishvirtuallibrary.org/jsource/History/Diaspora.html

23. Flavius Josephus, *The wars of the Jews*

24. *Holy Bible*, King James Version, Book of Deuteronomy;

25. *Holy Bible*, King James Version, Book of Ezekiel; Chapter 37

26. *Holy Bible*, King James Version, Book of Luke; Chapter 21

27. Blood Moon Rapture, http://www.redmoonrapture.com/crucifixion

28. Jewish Virtual Library, "Six Day War," http://www.jewishvirtuallibrary.org/jsource/History/67_War.html

29. Ibid.

30. Ibid.

31. Ibid.

32. Ibid.

33. *Holy Bible*, King James Version, Book of Luke; Chapter 21

34. *Holy Bible*, King James Version, Book of Joel; Chapter 2

35. Space.com, NASA Fireball Website Launches with New Russian Meteor Explosion Details," http://www.space.com/20216-russian-meteor-nasa-fireball-website.html

36. Bob King, *Universe Today*, "The Year of the Comets: Three Reasons Why 2013 Could be the Best Ever," February 19, 2013 http://www.universetoday.com/100049/the-year-of-the-comets-three-reasons-why-2013-could-be-the-best-ever/

37. FoxNews.com, "2013 comet may be brightest ever seen," January 13, 2013, http://www.foxnews.com/science/2013/01/13/comet-2013-among-brightest-ever-seen/

Chapter Six—Wars and Rumors of Wars

1. Stuart Winer and David Shamah, *Times of Israel*, "Stuxnet virus attacked Iran earlier than thought," February 27, 2013, http://www.timesofisrael.com/stuxnet-virus-attacked-iran-earlier-than-thought/

2. Jim Finkle, Reuters, "Researchers say Stuxnet was deployed against Iran in 2007," February 26, 2013, http://www.reuters.com/assets/print?aid=USBRE91P0PP20130226

3.   Daniel Terdiman, Cnet.com, "Stuxnet delivered to Iranian nuclear plant on thumb drive," April 12, 2013, http://news. cnet.com/8301-13772_3-57413329-52/stuxnet-delivered-to-iranian-nuclear-plant-on-thumb-drive/

4.   NBC News, "Iran condemned after over claim 'cancerous tumor' Israel has no place in Mideast," http://worldnews.nbcnews. com/_news/2012/08/18/13345717-iran-condemned-after-over-claim-cancerous-tumor-israel-has-no-place-in-mideast?lite

5.   Wikipedia, "Mahmoud Ahmadinejad and Israel," http:// en.wikipedia.org/wiki/Mahmoud_Ahmadinejad_and_Israel

6.   www.IsraelIran.net, "Israel threatening Iran," http://israeliran.net/

7.   Colin Kahl, Www.*WashingtonPost*.com, "Before attacking Iran, Israel should learn from its 1981 strike on Iraq," http://articles. washingtonpost.com/2012-03-02/opinions/35450430_1_ nuclear-weapons-israeli-strike-tuwaitha

8.   Daveed Gartenstein-Ross and Joshua Goodman, www. JewishPolicyCenter.org, "The Attack on Syria's al-Kibar Nuclear Facility," http://www.jewishpolicycenter.org/826/the-attack-on-syrias-al-kibar-nuclear-facility

9.   David Thornton, *Examiner.com*, "Iran's Apocalyptic Vision," http:// www.examiner.com/article/iran-s-apocalyptic-vision

10.   CNN.com, "Journalist: U.S. planning for possible attack on Iran," http://www.cnn.com/2005/ALLPOLITICS/01/16/ hersh.iran/

11.   YnetNews.com, "Peres: Iran nuclear policy could backfire," http://www.ynetnews.com/ articles/0,7340,L-3248543,00.html

12.   Ina Black, *The Guardian*, "Iran threat: we will burn American navy and set Israel alight if attacked, says Khamenei aide," http:// www.guardian.co.uk/world/2008/jul/09/iran.nuclear

13. *Haaretz.com*, "Israel threat to attack Iran is not a bluff, deputy FM says," http://www.haaretz.com/news/israel-threat-to-attack-iran-is-not-a-bluff-deputy-fm-says-1.4639

14. Robert Berger, CBS News, 'Hagel announces new U.S. arms sales to Israel amid fears over possible war with Iran," http://www.cbsnews.com/8301-202_162-57580703/hagel-announces-new-u.s-arms-sales-to-israel-amid-fears-over-possible-war-with-iran/

15. David Sanger, www.*NYTimes*.com, "On Carrier in Gulf, Cheney Warns Iran," http://www.nytimes.com/2007/05/11/world/middleeast/11cnd-cheney.html?_r=0

16. Matthew Cole and Mark Schone, Who is Killing Iran's Nuclear Scientists?" July 26, 2011 http://abcnews.go.com/Blotter/killing-irans-nuclear-scientists/story?id=14152453

17. Haaretz.com, "Sunday Times: Mossad agents behind Iran scientist assassination," January 16, 2012, http://www.haaretz.com/news/diplomacy-defense/sunday-times-mossad-agents-behind-iran-scientist-assassination-1.407593

18. Kurt Nimmo, www.InfoWars.com, "Chuck Hagel Green Lights Israeli Attacks On Syria and Iran," http://www.infowars.com/chuck-hagel-green-lights-israeli-attacks-on-syria-and-iran/

19. CBS News, "Hagel announces new U.S. arms sales to Israel amid fears over possible war with Iran," http://www.cbsnews.com/8301-202_162-57580703/hagel-announces-new-u.s-arms-sales-to-israel-amid-fears-over-possible-war-with-iran/

20. Daniel Serwer, Reuters, "Will this be the year that Israel goes to war with Iran?" January 3, 2013, http://blogs.reuters.com/great-debate/2013/01/03/will-this-be-the-year-that-israel-goes-to-war-with-iran/

21. Naveed Alam, *The Express Tribune*, "Is war between Israel and Iran inevitable," http://blogs.tribune.com.pk/story/16321/is-war-between-israel-and-iran-inevitable/

22. Alakhbar, "Israeli general: 5,000 Hezbollah warheads can hit Tel Aviv," http://english.al-akhbar.com/print/15383

23. Mark Mazzetti and Thom Shanker, *The New York Times*, "U.S. War Game Sees Perils of Israeli strike Against Iran," March 19, 2012, http://www.nytimes.com/2012/03/20/world/middleeast/united-states-war-game-sees-dire-results-of-an-israeli-attack-on-iran.html?pagewanted=all&_r=0

24. Jonathan Marcus, BBC.com, "Analysis" How would Iran respond to an Israeli attack?" http://www.bbc.co.uk/news/world-middle-east-17261265

25. Wikipedia, "List of Wars involving Israel," http://en.wikipedia.org/wiki/List_of_wars_involving_Israel

26. Ibid.

27. *Holy Bible*, King James Version, Book of Matthew; Chapter 24

28. Joshua Goldstein and Steven Pinker, *The New York Times*, "War Really Is Going Out of Style," December 17, 2011, http://www.nytimes.com/2011/12/18/opinion/sunday/war-really-is-going-out-of-style.html

29. John Mueller, Department of Political Science, Ohio state University, "The Demise of War and of Speculations About the Causes Thereof," February 7, 2007

30. Joshua Goldstein and Steven Pinker, *The New York Times*, "War Really Is Going Out of Style," December 17, 2011, http://www.nytimes.com/2011/12/18/opinion/sunday/war-really-is-going-out-of-style.html

Chapter 7—The Coming Mideast Crisis

1. Oren Kessler, *The Jerusalem Post*, "Egypt Islamist vows global caliphate in Jerusalem," August 5, 2012, http://www.jpost.com/Middle-East/Egypt-Islamist-vows-global-caliphate-in-Jerusalem

2. Huff Post, "Turkey Is Seeking Leadership of the Islamic World," November 5, 2012, http://www.huffingtonpost.com/ed-koch/turkey-is-seeking-leaders_b_2078869.html

3. BBC, "Turkey Timeline, A chronology of key events," http://www.bbc.co.uk/news/world-europe-17994865

4. Headquarters, United States European Command, "Turkey," http://www.eucom.mil/mission/the-region/turkey?print

5. www.TheOttomans.org, History, http://www.theottomans.org/english/history/index.asp

6. Joseph Puder, Front Page Magazine, "The Obama-Erdogan Alliance," August 6, 2012, http://frontpagemag.com/2012/joseph-puder/the-obama-erdogan-alliance/

7. David Ignatius, *Washington Post*, "Obama's friend in Turkey," June 7, 2012, http://articles.washingtonpost.com/2012-06-07/opinions/35459692_1_obama-and-erdogan-obama-erdogan-turkish-leader

8. *Hurriyet Daily*, "Obama names Turkish PM Erdogan among trusted friends," January 20, 2012, http://www.hurriyetdailynews.com/obama-names-turkish-pmerdogan-among-trusted-friends.aspx?pageID=238&nid=11897

9. CBN, "Obama Invites Netanyahu Back to Washington," http://www.cbn.com/cbnnews/insideisrael/2010/May/Obama-Extends-Invitation-to-Netanyahu/?Print=true

10. Reuters, "Netanyahu says Iran hasn't crossed nuclear "red

line," http://www.reuters.com/article/2013/04/29/us-iran-nuclear-israel-idUSBRE93S0IQ20130429

11.   Ed Koch, *Yonkers Tribune*, "Ed Koch Commentary: President Obama's Hostility to Israel Continues," http://yonkerstribune.typepad.com/yonkers_tribune/2011/05/ed-koch-commentary-president-obamas-hostility-to-israel-continues-by-ed-koch-.html

12.   Charles Krauthammer, *Washington Post*, "What Obama Did to Israel," http://www.washingtonpost.com/opinions/what-obama-did-to-israel/2011/05/26/AGJfYJCH_story.html

13.   Bret Stephens, *The Wall Street Journal*, "An Anti-Israel President," May 24, 2011 http://online.wsj.com/article/SB10001424052702304066504576341212934894494.html

14.   John Cassidy, *The New Yorker*, "Why is Obama Being So Friendly to Netanyahu?" March 20, 2013, http://www.newyorker.com/search/query?keyword=barack%20obama

15.   Ibid.

16.   CBS News, "Hagel announces new U.S. arms sales to Israel amid fears over possible war with Iran," http://www.cbsnews.com/8301-202_162-57580703/hagel-announces-new-u.s-arms-sales-to-israel-amid-fears-over-possible-war-with-iran/

17.   Yaakov Lappin, *Jerusalem Post*, "Hagel: Israel has right to decide on Iran strike," April 21, 2013, http://www.jpost.com/Defense/Hagel-Israel-has-right-to-decide-on-Iran-strike-310555

18.   Ibid.

19.   Kurt Nimmo, www.InfoWars.com, "Chuck Hagel Green Lights Israeli Attacks On Syria and Iran," http://www.infowars.com/chuck-hagel-green-lights-israeli-attacks-on-syria-and-iran/

20.   Jodi Rudoren and Isabel Kershner, *The New York Times*, "Airstrikes Tied to Israel May Be Message to Iranians," http://www.nytimes.

com/2013/05/06/world/middleeast/strikes-in-syria-linked-to-israel-may-be-a-signal-to-iran.html?pagewanted=all&_r=0

21. Associated Press, "Iran nuclear chief touts 3,000 new centrifuges"

22. Blood Moon Rapture, http://www.redmoonrapture.com/crucifixion

23. Jonathan Marcus, BBC, "Analysis: How would Iran respond to an Israeli attack?" March 6, 2012, http://www.bbc.co.uk/news/world-middle-east-17261265

24. Ibid.

25. Ibid.

26. Ibid.

27. Ibid.

28. Ibid.

29. Ibid.

Chapter Eight—Never Waste a Crisis

30. Kennedy Hickman, About.com Military History, "Spanish-American War: USS Maine Explodes," http://militaryhistory.about.com/od/navalbattles1800s/p/ussmaine.htm

31. Ibid.

32. Department of the Navy—Naval History and Heritage Command, "Tonkin Gulf Crisis, August 1964," http://www.history.navy.mil/faqs/faq120-1.htm

33. Peter Baker, *Washington Post*, 9/11 Linked To Iraq, In Politics if Not in Fact," September 12, 2007, http://www.washingtonpost.com/wp-dyn/content/article/2007/09/11/AR2007091102316.html

34. Roosevelt Institute, "The New Deal," http://rooseveltinstitute.org/policy-and-ideasroosevelt-historyfdr/new-deal

35. Tim Worstall, *Forbes*.com, "Did WWII Really End the Great Depression? Perhaps Not" July 2/2012, http://www.forbes.com/sites/timworstall/2012/07/02/did-wwii-really-end-the-great-depression-perhaps-not/

36. Pete Harrison, Reuters, "Never waste a good crisis, Clinton says on climate," March 7, 2009, http://www.forbes.com/sites/timworstall/2012/07/02/did-wwii-really-end-the-great-depression-perhaps-not/

37. Ibid.

38. Jonah Goldberg, *LA Times*.com, "Obama's fear-mongering," March 10, 2009, http://www.latimes.com/news/opinion/commentary/la-oe-goldberg10-2009mar10,0,6414638.column

39. Gerald Seib, *The Wall Street Journal*, "In Crisis, Opportunity for Obama," November 21, 2008, http://online.wsj.com/article/SB122721278056345271.html

40. Ibid.

41. CNN.com, "Obama warns of turning crisis into a catastrophe," http://www.cnn.com/2009/POLITICS/02/04/stimulus/

42. Ibid.

43. Simmi Aujla, Politico, "GOP: Obama using oil crisis to push cap and trade," June 15, 2010, http://www.politico.com/news/stories/0610/38549.html

44. Jonathan Capehart, *Washington Post*, "Pelosi defends her infamous health care remark," June 20, 2012, http://www.politico.com/news/stories/0610/38549.html

45. Townhall.com, "Sandy Hook: Obama's Latest Crisis To Exploit," January 18, 2013, http://townhall.com/columnists/davidlimbaugh/2013/01/18/sandy-hook-obamas-latest-crisis-to-exploit-n1491937/page/full

46. Tzvi Ben-Gedalyahu, *Jewish Press*, "PA Official" If We Had a Nuke, We'd Use It This Morning," May 9, 2013, http://www.jewishpress.com/news/pa-official-if-we-had-a-nuke-wed-use-it-this-morning-video/2013/05/09/

47. Ibid.

Chapter Nine—A Treaty with Many

1. Leland Vittert, FoxNews.com, "Obama's Speech Sends Chills Through Netanyahu Government," May 19, 2011, http://www.foxnews.com/world/2011/05/19/obamas-speech-met-surprise-israel/

2. Charles Krauthammer, *WashingtonPost*.com, "What Obama did to Israel," May 26, 2011 http://www.washingtonpost.com/opinions/what-obama-did-to-israel/2011/05/26/AGJfYJCH_story.html

3. Louis Charbonneau, Reuters, "Palestinians win implicit U.N. recognition of sovereign state," November 29, 2012, http://www.reuters.com/article/2012/11/29/us-palestinians-statehood-idUSBRE8AR0EG20121129

4. Ethan Bronner, *The New York Times*, "Palestinians Restate Demands to Netanyahu," April 17, 2012, http://www.nytimes.com/2012/04/18/world/middleeast/palestinians-deliver-letter-on-peace-talks-to-netanyahu.html?_r=0

5. Office of the United Nations Special Coordinator For The Middle East Peace Process, Ad Hoc Liaison Committee, Brussels, 19 March 2013

6. Ibid.

7. Robert McMahon and Jonathan Masters, Council on Foreign Relations, "Palestinian Statehood at the UN," November 30, 2012, http://www.cfr.org/palestinian-authority/palestinian-statehood-un/p25954

8. Louis Charbonneau, Reuters, "Palestinians win implicit U.N. recognition of sovereign state," November 29, 2012, http://www.reuters.com/article/2012/11/29/us-palestinians-statehood-idUSBRE8AR0EG20121129

9. Ibid.

10. Haaretz.com, "Report: Obama promised Abbas a Palestinian state within two years," April 29, 2010, http://www.haaretz.com/news/diplomacy-defense/report-obama-promised-abbas-a-palestinian-state-within-two-years-1.287415

11. Ibid.Barak Ravid, Haaretz.com, "Obama: Netanyahu doesn't understand Israel's best interests, driving it into international isolation," January 15, 2013, http://www.haaretz.com/blogs/diplomania/obama-netanyahu-doesn-t-understand-israel-s-best-interests-driving-it-into-international-isolation.premium-1.494088

12. Haaretz.com, Associated Press Report, "Kerry: Israelis and Palestinians have two years to make peace," April 17, 2013, http://www.haaretz.com/news/diplomacy-defense/kerry-israelis-and-palestinians-have-two-years-to-make-peace-1.516040

13. Agence France-Presse-Jerusalem, "Israel hails Arab League's stance on land swaps," http://www.hurriyetdailynews.com/israel-hails-arab-leagues-stance-on-land-swaps.aspx?pageID=238&nid=45932

Chapter Ten—The Sequence of Prophetic Events

1. David Brennan, *The Israel Omen*, (New Orleans, Teknon Publishing, 2009)

2. Ibid.

3. Ibid.

4. TimeandDate.com, "Asteroid to fly by Earth," February 14, 2013, http://www.timeanddate.com/astronomy/asteroid-near-earth.html

5. Space.com, "NASA Fireball Website Launches with New Russian Meteor Explosion Details," http://www.space.com/20216-russian-meteor-nasa-fireball-website.html

6. Bob King, *Universe Today*, "The Year of the Comets: Three Reasons Why 2013 Could be the Best Ever," February 19, 2013 http://www.universetoday.com/100049/the-year-of-the-comets-three-reasons-why-2013-could-be-the-best-ever/

7. Ibid.

8. Joe Rao, Space.com, "The 9 Most Brilliant Comets Ever Seen," October 5, 2012, http://www.space.com/17918-9-most-brilliant-great-comets.html

9. FoxNews.com, "2013 comet may be brightest ever seen," January 13, 2013, http://www.foxnews.com/science/2013/01/13/comet-2013-among-brightest-ever-seen/

10. Brian Williams, NBC Nightly News, "A Comet To Watch In 2013," http://www.nbc.com/news-sports/msnbc-video/2012/10/a-comet-to-watch-in-2013/

11. David Brennan, *The Israel Omen*, (New Orleans, Teknon Publishing, 2009)

12. Blood Moon Rapture, http://www.redmoonrapture.com/crucifixion

13. Ibid.